Ischia (Isola d'Ischia) Island Tourism Italy.

Discovery and Leisure

Author
Aiden Taylor

Published
By
Information-Source.
16192 Coastal Highway Lewes,
DE 19958. USA.

.

Table of Content

Ischia (Isola d'Ischia) Island
Introduction

Ischia lies in magnificent beauty in the Gulf of Naples, beyond Procida and across the bay from Napoli. The third most populated Italian island after Sicily and Sardinia. Ischia has volcanic origins, formed after a long series of eruptions lasted something like 150,000 years.

Larger than Capri, its distinctive lofty Mount Epomeo is a massive green tuft rising at the center; it benefits the whole island with mild climatic conditions all over the year. The average temperature is 18°C even in winter, and 35°C in August, the hottest month.

That volcanic activity endowed the island with the thermal bathsthat have been renowned since ancient times.

The Romans brought profitably out the natural thermal springs, as demonstrated by the votive tablets found near Nitrodi's spring in Barano d'Ischia, where there used to be a small temple dedicated to Apollo and the nymphs, Nitrodie (waters' protectors).

Originally called Isle of Pinthecusa, the traces of the ancient thermae publicae were destroyed; that coupled with the fall of the Roman Empire meant the curative springs were forgotten about until the Renaissance. Thanks to a geology professor, Dr Giulio Iasolino, at the

University of Naples (end of XVI century), who wrote a treatise about the natural remedies of the island, the hot springs fell into favor again. The island by this time had been re-dubbed Ischia.

By the beginning of the 17th century, the reputation of thermal therapies and their curative powers became widely popular; a group of noble Neapolitan philanthropists built "Pio Monte della Misericordia" a huge free access thermal establishment in Casamicciola. Since then, many impressive resorts have been built through the centuries, making Ischia an international landmark for tourists coming to cure their diseases, along with the island's beautiful nature and sea.

In the Iliad, there is a famous phrase written on Nestore's cup (found close to Montevico Lacco Ameno) that sings the praises of the local wine. The Ancient Euboaens, that colonized the island, introduced the production of the nectar of the gods and a special technique to cultivate it. You will find vineyards everywhere in the island, planted on terraced land. You should definitely taste some of the vintages grown in the mineral-infused soil. The Biancolella is a stand-out white, while the Piedirosso is the island's excellent red.

There are several towns scattered about the island, each distinctive and charming. You will love walking through the narrow streets of this paradise and discovering the allures of each one.

Visit Villa La Colombaia and Giardini La Mortella in Forio d'Ischia, the Aragonese Castle in Ischia Ponte, Maroni beach in Barano d'Ischia, the volcanic promontory of Cretaio in Casamicciola Terme, the gorgeous Borgo Sant'Angelo in Serrara Fontana, and the splendid view of the touristic port from Lacco Armeno: you won't forget any of them!

Discover attractions in Ischia

About Isola d'Ischia

Ischia, the island of regeneration, of energies, of beauty and history. This casket of delights however has been looted, desecrated and subject to innumerable abuses over the years. This history of misuse continues into the present, as the lure of the quick buck continues to play its role in illegal building projects, damaging the land and the environment.

Ischia's history is littered with owners and sub owners who have seized, lost and re seized the island, often to the bewilderment of its inhabitants and the detriment of its terrain. However, despite the scars strewn across its past, Ischia has an abiding beauty and attraction, due to its riches in natural resources. The island has a unique supply of hot springs, spas, volcanic mud and valuable minerals.

Thus healing and renewal have become a resource by which the Island has recovered its economy and found its zenith as a centre of well being for countless visitors.

It is the largest of the three islands off the coast of Naples, (Procida, Capri and Ischia), and more than holds its own in this trinity of beauty rising from the azure waters of the Tyrrhenian Sea. This haven seems a million miles away from the haranguing, energy charged streets of Naples, (in reality only a short ferry journey away) and holds pleasures for the most intrepid or timid of travellers.

Fourty kilometres of coastline offer ample opportunities for sun-soaked relaxation. Inland, mountainous terrain awaits those who enjoy climbing. The peaceful pleasure of the fertile rolling volcanic hills offer less energetic strollers the chance to gain an advantageous view of the island without running short of breath. For the more urban minded visitor there is the elegant, traffic free town of

Sant'Angelo with its characteristic boutiques, local pottery and hand-crafted merchandise.

Nearby *Forio* is known for its bars and tree lined Boulevards, while the Port of Ischia for ferries from the metropolis of Naples, offers discotheques, and high street shopping. Ischia port is also famous for the imposing Aragon's castle, rich with tales of blood and thunder. In the past, the castle was the town itself, housing 1900 families, various religious orders and 13 churches. The castle served as a refuge and defence against the regular pirate attacks with which the island had been plagued in former days. It is now a fascinating museum. Whatever type of pastime is preferred, there is therapeutic mud, spas, springs and cures a plenty guaranteed to relax, creating space from the relentless onward march of twentieth century life as we know it.

Ischia's history is as rich and as varied as its climate and natural properties, beginning with the Greeks, who colonised the island in the eighth century B.C. naming it *Pithecusa* which translated means "monkey", in reference to the prevalence of these animals on the island in ancient times. Unlike today, the volcano was active. Possibly because of an eruption, the island was abandoned by the original inhabitants, and the more temperate town of Cuma was founded on the mainland.

Ischia was then resettled by Neapolitans, whose explosive character perhaps suited its volcanic activity. In 474 B.C., Hiero of Syracuse warred against the Etruscans and as part of a quest to fortify the whole of Naples, leaving a garrison on Ischia and plans for a castle to protect the capital city of the island (also known as Ischia). He emerged victorious from battle and the castle was built.

In 6 A.D., after his visit to Capri, the emperor Augustus, desperate to obtain the Island, swapped it with Naples for Ischia, which once again fell into Neapolitan hands. However well defences had proved in earlier days, they were ineffective in the face of Romans might some centuries later, and in 322 B.C. the Romans conquered and took Naples and Ischia.

The list of invaders since then is daunting. The first swathe, apart from the steady stream of marauding pirates, included the Heruli, Ostrogoths, Byzantines, Saracens and Normans, who heralded what some refer to as the "first Renaissance" under Roger II. The Normans were followed by Roger II's grandson, Swabian Frederick II, whose mother was a Norman and his father was Henry VI, Duke of Swabia. His reign, for the most part, was peaceful, following the tolerant and eclectic view of government Roger II had begun.

The Angevins who had left their mark, with papal support, on Campania and Sicily, were followed for a time by Alfonso V of Aragon, who in 1441, reconstructed the ancient Greek fort on a grand scale transforming it into the grand castle it is today and which quickly became the scene of many fights, and transference of power.

Under Aragon rule, Alfonso V, proclaimed the island a colony for the Spanish Kingdom of Castiglia. He then built a bridge connecting the castle and its inhabitants with the world beyond its walls to the rest of the island.

By 1550, the threat of invasion by Pirates and the warlike Pisans had abated, and the population shifted from its coastal watch towers, to more comfortable terrain further inland, forming the beginning of what is now the town of Ischia. In its present form the town has six communes, or administrative areas. From where, though the beach has always been accessible, it was no longer of central importance. Throughout this period Ischia was fraught with strife slipping and falling from the hands of the Durres into Anjou power (who had returned since the days of the house of

Aragon), and back again, as the rival houses squabbled for possession of the jewel of the Mediterranean.

By the 1700's, the Bourbon's were in custody of the island which in 1806 fell into French possession till it fell prey to the English, in pursuit of the French. Finally a devastating earthquake interrupted, scattering intruders.

Ischia finally found tranquility in modernity, and since the invention of the Grand Tour has been subjected to nothing worse than invasions of fleets of tourists, exploring the island on the picturesque three wheeled *microtaxis* equipped for touring. These visitors are for the most part German, a large number of whom stay on the island permanently, enriching Ischia's coffers and enjoying its unique pleasures.

Unfortunately, owing to a combination of earthquakes and irregular building projects, very few traditional houses remain intact. Those which have escaped demolition are connected to agriculture, or small coastal enterprises such as fishing. Sant'Angelo is a fishing community and has remained largely untouched.

Typical ancient houses were constructed of stone or carved tuff, such as those found on Mount Epomèo, the highest mountain on the Island. Its name, translated from the Greek means "look around" due to the marvellous views to be had from its heights. The top 75 meters of the peak are bedaubed in volcanic ash, as the mountain, though not volcanic itself, is a result of eruptions from other vents on the island. To avoid excess damage from falling roofs in case of an earthquake or further volcanic activity, roofs of dwellings are created from the lightweight lava "*lapilli*", largely constituted of volcanic ash, are beaten with sticks and poles till they become a thin waterproof crust. Upon the completion of a house, tradition dictates that a party be held with music dancing and a veritable feast of fine fare.

Regular damage to buildings through earthquakes over the centuries have given rise to different styles of housing, ranging from Baroque to Liberty dotted across the island.

The recently renowned garden of La Mortella, has added depth, appeal and style to Ischia, perhaps symbolising the recent flowering of this beautiful if beleaguered island. Created and commissioned by the wife of the late English musician William Walton, La Mortella, winner of the "Best Italian Garden Award" is to be seen to be believed. As well as the stunning hotel, and the offer of refreshment to travellers, if opening hours are adhered to, relaxation in the cool of the garden, surrounded by flora and fauna from every corner of the globe from Zen to the tropics is there to be enjoyed. The garden and its owner, host countless concerts and cultural events.

This "Eden within Eden", surrounded by the brilliant blue of the wide ocean is home to rare coral and dolphins, and soon to become a protected area under the name of "*Reign of Neptune*" bathed in blissful weather and blessed with breathtaking sunsets, it is a spectacle of colour and a myriad types of life-aquatic and terrestrial.

Particularly picturesque is Forio, where the Sunset creates an optical illusion of a horizontal green ray. In times past, women would stand beneath this mystic light, praying for the safe return of their husbands from the sea. Waiting at evening for the sight of homecoming vessel silhouetted against the horizon through the shimmering green vale of light, as they returned to the island at dusk.

The mysteries of the sea around the island may now be enjoyed by any traveller who wishes to rent a *taxi boat* and go exploring. There are any fascinating destinations along the strips of beach around the island, not least of which is an area on the beach which reaches a temperature of 100 degrees!

All these beauties are to be discovered and enjoyed and were immortalised forever in the classic film "Cleopatra", which was filmed on the Island, and perhaps inspired something of the passion between Richard Burton and Elizabeth Taylor.

Sant'Angelo d'Ischia

Sant'Angelo is a splendid fishing village, perhaps the most beautiful on the island. It can be reached exclusively on foot; which contributes significantly to preserving this place, which seems to have remained unspoilt as it used to be, with the sea life being lived on the narrow jetty. It is in an enchanting position, between two bays formed by a spit of sand.

The houses are still typical fishermen's houses, which seem to fit into one another, in the typical whitewash of Mediterranean villages, separated only by winding narrow streets. In piazzetta Trofa the houses close into a circle giving life to the centre of the bay.

But at night time the life of the fishermen gives way to the club and bar life, while the harbour becomes the mooring point for luxurious boats and the bay is transformed into the most fashionable and exclusive place on the island.

Today this is a particularly sought-after destination for tourists, many of whom stay permanently on the island. For the laziest the beauty spots of the island can be admired from the picturesque "microtaxis", three-wheeled vehicles fitted out for sightseeing tours. The traditional houses left intact are very few and are closed in by building speculation, but the few remaining ones still have features related to the occupation of the inhabitants: those inland are linked to agriculture, while those on the coast are linked to fishing.

The typical houses are built in stone or carved in the rock (tuff), like those on mount Epomèo, with the roofs made, to make them lighter, in a material obtained by striking lava stone with large sticks. When the building of a house, which involved all the neighbours, was finished, a big celebration was organised with music, dancing, singing and plenty of food. Continuous destruction by earthquakes has however given the island its present appearance, with baroque and liberty style buildings alongside rural houses.

The Mortella is the splendid garden created by the wife of the English composer William Walton. As well as offering cool shelter to travellers, it offers the maximum relaxation among plants from every corner of the planet in a variety of settings, including also a zen garden. The gardens are completely devoid of architectural barriers and host countless concerts and cultural events.

The sea around the island is a spectacle of colours and underwater life and is soon to become a protected marine area, named the "Kingdom of Neptune". From seaweeds to dolphins to coral, everything contributes to making the seabed an underwater paradise.

Particularly picturesque is the landscape that can be enjoyed form the Forio Point, where the sunset creates a unique, inexplicable optical illusion, a green light on the horizon, and where the women of the island used to wait for their husbands who had gone to sea, praying that they might appear soon on the horizon.

The taxi boats that can be hired on the island enable you to discover mysterious, interesting places, like the stretch of beach where the sand becomes as hot as 100°C, due to a strange phenomenon!

The beauty of the island was immortalised in Cleopatra, filmed at an enormous cost on Ischia, which was also the beginning of the love affair between *Liz Taylor* and *Richard Burton*.

Ischia volcanic History

Ischia is an island lying off the Gulf of Napoli, some 30 km WSW from Napoli, 35 km west from Vesuvio and about 8 km from the mainland coast at Capo Miseno. Its highest peak, Epomeo, is not a volcano (as which it is frequently described), but is made up of an uplifted and tilted block (horst) of green ash-flow tuff (possibly erupted from Campi Flegrei). Numerous youthful and historic eruptive centers are scattered on its flanks, the most recent of which is Arso, formed in 1302 (or 1301). Continuing volcano-tectonic activity was destructively demonstrated on 28 July 1883, when the famous thermal resort of Casamicciola was levelled by the most violent in a series of local earthquakes, killing more than 2213 people.

Numerous eruptions from various sites have occurred on Ischia during the past 2500 years, indicating that the island is volcanically active and may well erupt in the future. Ground deformation (uplift, subsidence and tilting) are continuing to the present day. It is very likely that a shallow magma body is present below the island, causing these deformations. The reconstructed and/or documented style of eruption implies great hazards in the case of renewed activity.

Ischia, with a surface of about 46 km2, is the largest of the beautiful islands dotting the margins of the Gulf of Napoli, and it forms one of the most complex volcanoes of that region. Morphologically, it consists of the central-western highland (horst) of Epomeo which is surrounded by lower terrain punctuated by at least 40 volcanic centers. Most of these occur in the eastern half of the island, but a few are present in its SW and NW corners. Since the early 1980's, an old caldera of unknown age has been suspected below Ischia by Chiesa et al. (1985), whose relic moat is constituted by Castello di Ischia, Punta Imperatore, and possibly Monte di Vico, forming a half-ring around the southern circumference of the island. Rocks of the pre-existing volcanic complex are exposed mostly in the southern and SE parts of Ischia.

The earliest established event in the geologic history of Ischia is the cataclysmic eruption of the Green Tuff, dated at 0.74 +/-0.09 Ma by Capaldi et al. (1976-77) and much less, that is, 53 ka by Gillot et al. (1982) and Chiesa et al. (1985). This large-volume ash-flow tuff was erupted from a site yet to be identified and covers an area conservatively estimated at 300 km^2, including all of Ischia and the Campi Flegrei. Its maximum thickness (at Ischia? no precise info) is ca. 1000 m, and still exceeds 600 m in the Campi Flegrei; it was probably erupted in a series of large-scale explosive eruptions (Capaldi et al. 1976-77). Compositionally, the potassic alkali trachyte Green Tuff magma is typical for volcanic rocks in the Campanian area. The much younger eruption date given by the more recent sources is of great significance for the understanding of Ischia's volcanism and reflects much faster processes than previously thought.

The Green Tuff was either deposited subaqueously or submerged below sea-level soon after, as evidenced by the presence of

eruption occurred in the NE prolungation of an eruptive fissure of a prehistoric eruption that produced a tuff ring (of which the Fondo Ferraro and Costa del Lenzuolo are remains) and a thick trachytic lava flow. Initially, the Porto d'Ischia eruption was phreatic-phreatomagmatic, piercing through the prehistoric trachyte flow. Following this initial stage, new trachytic lava fragments and scoria were ejected. No lava emission occurred during this eruption. Soon after the end of the activity, the maar-type explosion crater was filled with water. Rittmann & Gottini (1981) believe that the Porto d'Ischia eruption is identical with the one described by (the younger?) Plinius. In that event, "flames" were ejected and much damage was done to a citadel. The eruption is said to have "transformed a plain into a lake" a scenario similar to that reconstructed for the Porto d'Ischia eruption.

Rotaro eruptions, -91 until ca. 300. The Monte Rotaro tephra cone and lava dome/flow complex formed by a series of eruptions, possibly coinciding with the historically documented eruptions of 91 BC and AD 69. The exact timing of the eruptive events is uncertain: Rittmann & Gottini (1981) describe Rotaro I as "prehistoric" while other sources attribute it to an eruption recorded for 91 BC (see, e.g., Krafft 1974). The Rotaro complex is a beautiful example of nested cones breached by lava effusion, located along an eruptive fracture that trends N20°ree;W. Also the dates of the later phases of the Rotaro eruptive sequence are uncertain. Rittmann & Gottini (1981) assume some date in the 3rd post-Christ century while Krafft (1974) gives AD 69 as the date (misprinted as 69 BC in the German translation of Krafft, 1974). Rittmann & Gottini (1981) point to the fact that Rotaro I is covered by tephra from the Montagnone-Maschiatta eruption (thought to have occurred around AD 140) while Rotaro II is not, neither are Rotaro III and IV. The entire sequence of Rotaro eruptions is here taken together even though it may to some extent overlap with the Montagnone-Maschiatta eruption.

In any case, Rotaro I was formed by an initial explosive phase with early lithic and later magmatic (pumice) tephra ejection, and successive large-volume lava extrusion. A major dome rose to about 340 m asl, with a short lava flow extending from its NW base. After the end of extrusion, a large (350 m diameter) pit crater

31

formed on the dome summit, it still has a depth of about 120 m today.

Monte Rotaro II began with powerful phreatic-phreatomagmatic explosions from a new vent on the NNW flank of the Rotaro I dome (about 300 m from the summit), represented by a basal breccia in the deposit from the eruption. Immediately after, pumice and ash were ejected before a new lava dome with a scoriaceous surface largely filled the new depression. At a later date ("several decades later", according to Krafft, 1974), a new explosive vent exploded through the N base of the Rotaro II dome, some 300 m NNW of the Rotaro II vent. Thus the crater of Rotaro III was formed, being much smaller than its predecessor. Most of the magma, during this eruptive episode, was erupted quietly, forming a small dome that extended northwards outside the vent and extended into the sea in a trachytic flow some 600 m long. In its most recent eruptive gasp, the Rotaro volcanic complex extruded a small lava flow (Rotaro IV; not Monte Tabor as written in Krafft, 1974 which is a much older volcanic formation), about 350 m long. This flow is distinguished from the Rotaro III flow for its distinctly more alkaline composition and resulting brighter color.

Montagnone-Maschiatta eruption, about AD 140. One of the most recent eruptions of Ischia occurred only about 1800 years ago, on the same eruptive fracture that had been the site of the prehistoric Fondo Ferraro and the ca. 150 BC Porto d'Ischia eruptions, right between those earlier eruption centers. Following the typical sequence of Ischian volcanic eruptions, the vent-clearing phase ejected abundant clasts of pre-existing rock, immediately followed by abundant pumice and ash that left a thick deposit in the NE part of the island.

After the explosive stage of the eruption, degassed viscous magma rose within the crater and formed a voluminous dome that overflowed the crater rim in the SW and NE, thus assuming an elliptical shape. Later, more fluid lava broke through the dome's carapace at its SE base and flowed in the direction of the later Arso crater. Due to this partial "emptying" of the dome's interior, the top of the protrusion collapsed, forming a pit crater.

Pottery found below the basal pumice of the Montagnone-Maschiatta eruption indicates an age of no earlier than the 2nd post-Christ century. Rittmann & Gottini (1981) cite as further evidence for a 2nd century eruption date the submersion of the ancient town of Aenaria, situated between the NE tip of Ischia and the Castello di Ischia. Pottery found among the ruins of that town, now 6.5 m below sea-level, indicates a date of about 130-140 AD for the event that led to its catastrophic submersion. This, according to Rittmann & Gottini (1981), occurred in response to the eruption at Montagnone-Maschiatta.

1302 Arso eruption. The most recent eruption on Ischia occurred during January or Feb 1302 (Krafft, 1984, gives 18 January 1301 as the beginning of this eruption), after about thousand years of volcanic inactivity on Ischia. It opened a new crater at a site named

Cremate and emitted a lava flow (named Arso) to the NE coast. Most info for the following summary derives from Rittmann & Gottini (1981).

Prior to the eruption, the site was known for its solfataric activity ("solfonaria"). Nothing is known about any precursory phenomena (but Newhall & Dzurisin, in Calderas, p. 119, cite reports of an earthquake preceding the eruption). The beginning of the eruption was sudden and violently explosive, phreatic or phreatomagmatic, as the hydrothermal system flashed into steam by some unknown depressurization process. The basal deposits of the 1302 eruption has abundant fragments of fumarolically altered rock, torn from the surface of the "solfonaria" geothermal site, and mixed with fragments of Rotaro and

Montagnone-Maschiatta pumice. Old written sources describe the fall of "ash mixed with sulfur". Inhabitants of the area must have been completely surprised by the disaster, leaving money and artefacts when trying to escape from settlements near the new vent. The eruption area was populated and Ischia Porto was only 1.5 km distant. The only escape way was across the sea. It was probably during this phase that "many" persons and animals were killed and great damage was done to inhabited and agricultural areas. Some deaths were apparently due to asphyxiation due to strong SO2 emission.

The phreatic or phreatomagmatic phase of the eruption was followed by the emission of large volumes of fresh pumice and ash, darkening the sky and causing ash falls to 300 km distant (location of distal fallout is not indicated by Rittmann & Gottini, 1981). The eastern part of Ischia including the town of Ischia Porto was buried under a deep cover of pyroclastics (no thickness data in Rittmann & Gottini, 1981). Then, a brief period of relative quiet ensued before more degassed and more mafic magma reached the surface. Very porous and large scoria were then ejected, building a tephra ring around the 500 m-wide crater.

During the final, least violent, but probably longest, phase of the eruption, viscous lava rose within the crater, first forming a dome that then overflowed the crater rim at its lowest point, on its SE side. Just east of the crater, the flow turned NE, pushing before it a part of the crater rim. The higher part of the descent was across steep terrain but nearing the shore, flatter terrain was encountered, causing the lateral extension of the flow. When the lava finally arrived at the coast, it entered the sea along a front about 1 km wide, displacing the coastline 200 m into the sea and creating a new headland (Capo Molino). This phase of the eruption lasted about 2 months. The final length of the flow is 2.7 km, and its average thickness 9 m, total volume is about 1.3×10^7 m^3.

Volcanic hazards. No volcanic eruptions have occurred on Ischia since about 700 years, but seismic activity (very intense in the 18th and 19th centuries) as well as continuing ground deformation point to magma movements at shallow depth. While subsidence occurs in the coastal areas of the island (which may correspond to the overall subsidence observed in many other places around the Gulf of Napoli, as noted by Newhall & Dzurisin, Calderas, p. 121), the central part with Epomeo continues to be uplifted. It would require more continuous and precise repeated measurements especially in the case of earthquakes to judge if the Epomeo uplift may correspond to the uprise of magma within the suggested shallow reservoir. Eruptions have occurred repeatedly during the past about 53 ka (after the eruption of the Green Tuff) and were particularly frequent during the period from about 500 BC until AD 300. During this period, the NE part of the island has been affected by a total of 5 significant eruptive events (Porto d'Ischia, Rotaro I, Montagnone-Maschiatta, Rotaro II, Rotaro III). There is no ground on which to place speculations whether these eruptions represent one major cycle, but it is evident that that period was much more volcanically active than the following 1700 years (with only one eruption).

Regarding future eruptions, the following points are of particular relevance: the eruption will likely occur from a new vent somewhere in the lower regions of the island, most probably in its NE sector,

like all recent major eruptions, the onset of activity is expected to be violently explosive and will result in the fall of very large, dense lithics followed by large volumes of pumice,

initial activity is likely to be influenced by the presence of ground or sea water. Surge clouds are a common feature of such eruptions and would extend to distances of several kilometers, a range within total destruction is to be expected.

A hazard which is even greater than that of renewed volcanic activity is that of earthquakes (because they usually have no predecessors). The history of Ischia knows of at least 5 destructive earthquakes that have also caused fatalities (1228: 700 deaths, probably in a landslide caused by the earthquake; 1796: 7 deaths; 1828: 28 deaths; 1881: 129 deaths; 1883: 2213 deaths). The shallow focus of the latest of these quakes and the very limited areas affected (the devastating 1883 temblor was not even felt on the nearby mainland) point to a connection between these events and movements of the Epomeo horst, maybe in response to magma movements in the postulated shallow reservoir. More geophysical studies are required in order to reveal the internal structure and processes of Ischia volcano.

Travel Guide

Sightseeing in Isola di Ischia what to see. Complete travel guide

Isola di Ischia is the biggest island in the Gulf of Naples. A lot of tourists are attracted there by thermal springs, but many consider the island as an option for its wonderful beaches. It's way less known that Isola di Ischia is also a focus of historical landmarks and cultural centers, which are worth visiting.

The most popular cultural center on the island is the Museo archeologico di Pithecusea. It retains an impressive collection of clay and bronze items; some of them are thousands of years old. The central point of the exhibition is the collection of huge clay jars.

The most important historical landmark of the island is certainly Castello Aragonese located on top of a rocky cliff. The very first fortification in its place has been built back in Antique age. The fortress was fully rebuilt in the Middle Ages; the structure retains this form until today. This massive and amazing building occupies about 550 square meters of space. There were 13 churches in its area, but all of them were raised by British conquerors in 19th century. Today tourist can only watch ruins of these religious buildings and visit castle halls open for public.

Cattedrale dell'Asswnta is an interesting religious landmark. It also took serious damage during the war with England, but its beautiful chapel with fine wall-paintings has survived until these days almost intact. There's also the museum dedicated to famous film director Luchino Visconti on the island. The venue occupies La Colombaia villa and houses a large collection of photos, onstage dresses and personal belongings of famous director.

Gardens of Isola di Ischia are permanent symbol of the island; walk around them would be an amazing activity. Charming La Mortella occupies two hectares area and hosts more than 3,000 varieties of plants, including very rare ones. Giardini Ravino is another attractive garden with beautiful living sculptures made of cacti.

Thermal healing springs have made island the popular vacation area; they are worth extra mentioning. The biggest and most beautiful thermal complex is the Giardini Poseidon Terme ; it is the world importance site. There are 18 pools set up for its guests.

Walking around picturesque towns of Isola di Ischia will be an unforgettable adventure regardless of the town chosen. There are lots of beautiful old houses everywhere and many of them host popular restaurants, shops and hotels. Fans of excursions will certainly like the capital city of Ischia Porto, as well as Lacco Ameno and Forio found nearby.

Unique thermal parks have become a true symbol of the island. Besides sources of thermal water, there are several pits with healing mud on the island. Nowadays, these parks have been turned into modern relaxation areas with up-to-date spa centers. In the past, only members of royal families could relax and rejuvenate in this region, but now everyone is welcome to spend several days in the thermal park and enjoy its unique healing properties.

Travelers interested in primarily in beach recreation will enjoy their free time at Marina dei Maronti. The length of this beach is roughly 3,000 meters. As the beach is so long, there are areas with a developed infrastructure and absolutely wild strips of sand with few people. Citara Beach is no less popular. This beach is located in a picturesque mountain region. It is the best choice for travelers craving for privacy and secluded atmosphere. By the way, it is easy to combine sunbathing and interesting short hikes on this part of the island. Within last decade, many modern sports centers appeared on the island, so travelers will easily find excellent tennis courts and equestrian schools.

Family trip with kids

Family trip to Isola di Ischia with children. Ideas on where to go with your child
Children, especially younger children, will surely like it here. If your child is active and loves adventure, take him to Indiana Park, which is located in Fiano. Here you can find 7 different routes and a 13-meters-high climbing wall. Even a child can walk most of the trails due to the adjustable height level. Your child can feel himself a real Indiana Jones or Lara Croft and, if he wants, he can improve his climbing skills there is a special wall for this, which is also suitable for children.

There are puppet theaters organized here for them, and a real electric train. However, the most exciting and interesting for the child in the park will be the opportunity to see the huge dinosaurs. Ancient monsters do not just stand still. When a child comes to a huge reptile, it "comes to life", starts moving and making sounds through built-in sensors. Such a spectacular view will impress any kid.

Climbing Mount Epomeo will be an exciting adventure for your child. It is best to do this with the staff of the "Epomeo in Sella" center, who suggest seeing all the natural beauties in the horse's or pony's saddle. If your child is four-legged friends will like, then safely go with him to the sports center "Aragona Arabians". Here, anyone can not only communicate with the neighbors, with whom we share the planet but also learn how to sit properly in the saddle and manage the horse. There are also classes for adults, so you won't have to sit aside, waiting while your child is riding a horse.

In Ischia, there is an opportunity to teach your child snorkeling, which is somewhat a simpler and more popular alternative to diving. Swimming with a mask and a tube has its own specifics but it is much easier to understand it than the nuances of handling all kinds of diving equipment. Both adults and children are taught snorkeling at the Associazione Nemo in a play form, allowing the kids to plunge into the admiration of the beauties of the natural world. If your child is old enough and he wants to try himself as a diver, then you can get training and a license and dive on the island.

A child might like the idea of visiting a thermal park. There are several of them on the island, children are allowed in each of them, with the condition of observing all the rules of conduct. Casamicciola, Poseidon Gardens, Aphrodite Gardens, Thermal Park Eden there are many places in Ischia, where you can rest and relax. If you want, you can get a snack without leaving the territory of the thermal park, there are cafes and restaurants in each of them, where both adults and children will enjoy the food.

Be sure to take your child to Aragonese castle. This majestic structure has remained till our days almost in its original form. The castle was built where an ancient fortification used to be. In addition to the magnificent view from its walls, the Aragonese Castle is famous for its especially large 550 sq.m. area and the ruins of

13 ancient churches, destroyed by the British in the 19th century. It is here that the child can truly plunge into history. It's one thing to read about the actions of the ancient kings in textbooks, and another one is to stand at a place that remembers sieges, feasts, and fights. A small child will certainly like to imagine himself a knight or a princess, the hero of one of his favorite cartoons.

Take your child to the Archaeological Museum of Pitekuza, whose exposition will allow you to get even better acquainted with the past of the island and see the artifacts, whose age is thousands of years old. The Botanical Garden of La Mortella will please young naturalists with a variety of plants, and the Ravino garden with the unusual sculptural compositions. With a child of any age, you can walk along the streets of Ischia-Porto, where you can literally feel the spirit of antiquity.

Top beaches

Vacation on Isola di Ischia beaches hidden bays, top resorts and recreation areas
Coastline of Isola di Ischia is the continuous series of twisted turns, capes and tiny bays with scenic quiet beaches. Beaches with natural mineral springs are the most popular. Vacations at these coastal sites allow combining leisure with healthcare.

Ischia is the one of the most popular resorts on the island. Its beaches are relatively small and most of them are covered with sand making them perfect places for rest with kids and for amazing activities. The resort is also surrounded with beautiful pine forests and cliffs.

Sant'Angelo beach is another stopping point for fans of picturesque landscapes. It's located next to the resort village of the same name. It's almost never crowded and has pretty calm sea. This sunny beach is popular among tourists who like to enjoy nature beauty in private ambience. Popular Cava Grado beach located nearby is known for its mineral springs. Tourists have to know that water at Cava Grado may be really hot, especially during spring high activity, so bathing should be taken with extra care.

San Francesco is worth mentioning among the well-equipped beaches. This part of the coast is full of entertainment places and charming restaurants. Most of beach visitors are tourists coming from popular resort hotels located nearby. This sand beach is an excellent choice for fans of active rest; younger travelers are attracted by special playgrounds set up for them.

Scenic Casamicciola Terme Bagnitiello sand beach is also known for its decent equipment; it's a very good choice for all-day-long rest. Its accessibility and a highway nearby are important advantages of this part of coast. Cartaromana beach is 300 meters long. It is considered one of the large-scale beaches of Isola di Ischia. It offers excellent view over Aragonese castle and is the perfect stop for diving enthusiasts. Hundreds of years ago, there was a large antique city on this shore. Nowadays, it has submerged into the sea and, thus, attracts a lot of divers. Healthcare tourism fans like Cartaromana beach for its mineral springs ensuring health-giving effect.

Lots of beautiful legends are associated with Citara beach; once it was considered that this part of the coast is protected by Venus. According to one of the legends, the high cliff at the coast is a petrified ship of Ulysses. Famous Giardini Poseidon Terme is a thermal complex located near this charming beach.

The biggest beach on the island is three kilometers long Maronti sand beach. Once it was popular among pirates, which hid their treasures there. Nowadays, this place attracts hundreds of tourists looking to enjoy beach vacations. Maronti provides everything for comfortable stay. There are various sports centers, equipment rental services and lots of nice restaurants and bars. Shallow San Montano beach covered with fine sand occupies a picturesque bay. It's a wonderful choice for tourists traveling with children.

Culture: sights to visit

Culture of Isola di Ischia. Places to visit old town, temples, theaters, museums and palaces

Be sure to visit Aragonese Castle, which is towering on the coastal rock near Ischia-Porte. The first construction on the site of this citadel was built in antiquity, and in the Middle Ages, the rulers of Ischia decided to strengthen and rebuild the fortress. Though the fortifications have suffered from time and weather since then, they still haven't lost their former greatness. It must be mentioned that the castle is really huge on the scale of the island It occupies the territory of 543 square meters. The height of the walls of the Aragonese stronghold exceeds one hundred meters. Needless to say that the view from the fortress is magnificent. On the territory of the Aragon castle, you can find the ruins of 13 churches, destroyed by the British in the 18th century.

The archaeological museum of Pithecuse will tell you the entire history of the island. A magnificent collection of artifacts from the ancient period is displayed here. Bronze statuettes, ceramics, household items, weapons, and equipment, presented in the museum, tell about the fate and hardships of the life of the first settlers of Ischia, who moved here before our era. However, the exposition also tells about later historical periods. Some evidence of Greek dominion can be found while strolling through the streets of Lacco Ameno resort town. Another historical museum is located near the church of St. Restituta.

If you want to find out about the old tradition of making ceramics, then go to the Menella factory. The dynasty of the potters, who own the production, origins from the Middle Ages. Therefore, the technology of making ceramic products used here can already be considered a historical value. If you want, you can not only learn how the factory produces ceramics, but also buy a souvenir to remember.

Not far from the resort town of Forio there is a place to visit not only for the fans of the architecture of bygone eras but also for movie admirers. This is the villa of Colombaia, which translates as "Dovecote". The famous Italian poet and public figure Luigi Patalano have built this beautiful white house in the 18th century. But the Dovecot is more known as the residence of the cult film director Luchino Visconti. Now it is the house-museum of the famous cinematographer. You can see about three hundred exhibits, one way or another related to the work of Visconti. Among them, there are scenery, costumes, awards, photos from the filming.

Another well-known place on the island is the Manzi Hotel. Luigi Manzi built it in 1863 next to the thermal spring of Gurgitello. The building of the hotel is valuable not only as an embodiment of the Italian architectural trends of the 19th century. Famous politicians, marquises, counts, industrialists and poets of bygone eras have stayed here. The well-known Giuseppe Garibaldi came to one of the hotel rooms to improve his health. The room where the hero of the unification of Italy lived, came to our days almost intact.

Take time to visit the Cathedral of Ischia. Next, to it, there is the beautiful Clock Tower, where the Museum of the Sea is located. Be sure to visit the Papal Basilica of the Madonna of Loreto and the Church of Saint Maria of the Snow of Soccorso in Forio. By the way, a dozen medieval towers that served to protect against the pirate raids have remained in the city. For a small fee, you can climb on Torrione, the highest of them. In the area of Fiiano there is an aqueduct of the times of Ancient Rome. In Casamecciola Terme, there is an interesting thermal center of Pio Monte della Misencordia, which was built in the 18th century. At the end of the 19th century, due to the earthquake, part of the buildings had to be restored, but the spirit of the era in this place is still strong.

Attractions & nightlife

City break in Isola di Ischia. Active leisure ideas for Isola di Ischia attractions, recreation and nightlife
Ischia attracts travelers not only with a rich historical past but also with a large selection of types of active pastime. For example, on the island, there are about a hundred diving centers, where for an affordable price they will teach you how to dive properly and will give an international diving license. By the way, due to multiple radon warm springs, whose water is mixed with the cold course, you can dive in the water area of Ischia not only from April to

October. Visibility is just great. One of the most popular places for diving is La Secca delle Formiche.

If you have a desire to observe the flora and fauna of the underwater world, and you do not want to spend money and time on diving training, then you can try snorkeling. There is a center in Ischia, where children and adults learn the peculiarities of snorkeling Associazione Nemo. You can rent equipment for wakeboarding or wake surfing on any major beach. If you want to increase your level of water skiing, it's worthwhile not only to rent them but also to learn to perform stunning tricks from local instructors. On the island, you can also ride a hydro cycle, a banana, and a water bike.

Ischia is also famous for its healing waters. At each major resort, you can find a thermal center, and even not one. Many local sources have been known since antiquity, so you do not only get rid of health problems when visiting the local baths but also touching the history. The oldest thermal park on the island is Castiglione at the Casamicciolo resort. are the Negombo Gardens in Lacco Ameno, the Poseidon Gardens in Forio and the pools of Apollo and Aphrodite in Serraro Fontana are known throughout the world for their waters.

Interestingly, this is the places where several springs emerge right off the coast. Their water, falling into the sea, forms true year-round warm pools. You can find such springs in the bays of Cafiero and Cartaromana. Asthma, rhinitis, gout, neuralgia, sinusitis, sciatica, tonsillitis, fibrositis, varicose veins, gynecological diseases these are just a few of the diseases that can be cured by healing baths. However, hypertensive patients, pregnant women, people with cardiovascular diseases and tuberculosis, better not be treated this way.

However, not only healing baths can diversify your leisure time on Ischia. There are tennis courts, football fields, and all conditions for playing handball or volleyball. Be sure to spend at least a couple of days on foot routes around the island. There are many routes here, so you should focus exclusively on your physical shape. You can climb Mount Epomeo, from which you will see a magnificent view, both on foot and on horseback, using the services of Epomeo in Sella, which revives the tradition of equestrian ascents. You can continue to communicate with horses in Aragona Arabians, where they will teach you how to sit in a saddle and give you the opportunity to ride a horse as long as you want.

Fans of clubs and parties will not be disappointed either. There are enough places for night parties on the island. The largest and most famous clubs in the capital are Calise and Ecstasy, which you can find on the central Via Roma. The disco New Valentino is also popular. Many coastal cafes and restaurants work till late at night, and after sunset, they organizing dance floors right under the open sky. The night bar and pub Kiwi Jam, English pub M9 Air Line, discos Jane and Harem deserve your attention. In general, after sunset, the real-life rages in Ischia Porto, and therefore the partiers should better go there.

Cuisine & restaurants

Cuisine of Isola di Ischia for gourmets.
Places for dinner best restaurants
Despite the fact that the culinary specialists in Ischia are true to many Italian cooking traditions, there are also their own unique courses, which you won't find in other places. One of the culinary "trademarks" of the island are Ischitanian rabbits with tomatoes. The animals are bred in special earth pits and are cooked in a special way. However, the variety of dishes from the local breed of rabbits is great. So if you do not like the version with tomatoes, look for any other variant of cooked rabbit in the menu.

Being surrounded by water from all sides, fish and seafood are very popular in Ischia. The best seafood courses you can find in the coastal restaurants, where the haul is always fresh. Tuna, gooseberry, king mackerel, squid, cuttlefish and sea urchin are fried, stewed, added to pizza, risotto, and salads. The mussels, which served with spicy sauce and as a separate dish, and as part of assorted seafood, and as part of many salads is also popular here. Those, who like fish will certainly not stay hungry.

Fans of pizza and pasta will find perhaps the best versions for these dishes in Ischia. No wonder many people think that in Campania they make the best pizza in the world. An important difference between local dishes and those, prepared in continental Italy, is the softer taste of vegetables and fruits, Among fruits, oranges, grapes, dates, cherries, fruits of the prickly pear and, of course, lemons are popular. The latter can be found in almost every dish in pasta, chocolate, and biscuits. Mostly because of the popularity of lemons on the island, the Limoncello liqueur gained a unique taste. Even convinced opponents of alcoholic beverages should taste it.

However, the chefs in Ischia use not only fruits but also vegetables. Tomatoes, potatoes, zucchini, artichokes, pepper all these are seasoned with basil, oregano or sage and served as a side dish or as a main course. Mushrooms, asparagus, and chestnuts are also often used in Ischia cuisine. Forest products here are usually served with rabbit meat, pork or beef. Be sure to try the local bread. It has its great taste because of the preserved old traditions of using wood-burning stoves for baking. Piennoli is an original local vegetable. It is small sweet and sour tomatoes, which you can buy at any market on the island.

The locals are rightly proud of their pastries. Even if you are indifferent to sweets, do not pass by a rum cake with a lemon liqueur. You can't find this cake in such a form anywhere else in the world. The taralli, a delicious dessert from strips of dough with almonds and pepper, are good for a snack. They usually sell taralli right on the streets. For those, who like sweets it is necessary to try mostaccioli, pastiera, rococo and chiacchiere. The latter, by the way, has its history since the days of Ancient Rome.

Biancolella, Ischia Bianco, Per'e Palummo and Ischia Rosso will ideally top up your meal, opening up the taste of the dishes from this island. Ischia is a real paradise for coffee admirers. The thing is, in this part of Italy until this day they still use the oldest methods of roasting coffee. Therefore, the taste of this drink on the island is truly unique. Local wines are also good. Wine-making originated in Ischia even before our era thanks to communication with the inhabitants of the Greek island of Evvoia. Now you can try some great types of wine here. Biancolella, Ischia Bianco, Per'e Palummo, and Ischia Rosso will perfectly complement any of your meals, rediscovering the taste of island cuisine in a new way.

Traditions & lifestyle

Colors of Isola di Ischia traditions, festivals, mentality and lifestyle

One of the characteristic features of the Italian mentality is the desire to always and in all circumstances adhere to the bella figura. You can translate this expression as "keep style". In fact, we are talking about certain conventions of public behavior. For example, no self-respecting Italian woman will even go out to buy bread without makeup or wearing home cloth. By the way, this tradition is the base of how the locals behave in public, which sometimes is taken for rudeness. The fact is that to any resident of Ischia it is important to show how strong, resolute and powerful he is, even if in reality it is not true and the situation does not require it. You just have to deal with it.

The most important thing for the Italians, in general, is not career or success, but getting pleasure from life. The pleasure can be different, but it is rarely associated with hard work, and therefore locals can seem somewhat lazy. It is because of the principle of obtaining pleasures from everything that the Italians are very sensitive to the process of eating. Delicious food and wine here are appreciated regardless of the cost.

Many travelers are sure that a vacation in Ischia with children is also good because of the attitude of the local residents. The fact is that for Italians the family is sacred, and the child can do anything he wants. That is why in a cafe there is always a highchair, and in the store, the seller can occupy a child with a toy. Even more reverent than for children is the attitude towards women. It is absolutely natural for the Italian men to admire the female beauty, regardless of her age. By the way, they get married quite late, and even after the wedding, the mother often remains in the first place for a man.

When you arrive in Ischia, you might think that the local people sometimes act too theatrically. Before supper, for example, the streets are filled with people, who are doing la passegiata. Beautiful clothes, a measured walk all this may seem posed, though this behavior is quite natural for an Italian. The aestheticism, typical for the residents of Ischia, manifests itself in everything. For example, the rickety hovel can be furnished with antique furniture inside. The locals use a lot of gestures, while talking, and do not hide emotions, but few people are ready to communicate with a stranger. But, if you are considered a friend then rest assured that many doors will now be open.

The inhabitants of Ischia are religious. The overwhelming majority of the population is Catholics, which, however, does not prevent them from being very superstitious. On the first week of September, they hugely celebrate the day of St. Giovanni Giuseppe on the Cross, who is the patron of not only the capital but together with St. Restità, the patron of the whole island. Fireworks, processions, dances, treats are all the obligatory parts of the celebration. The Day of the Holy Restrity from 16 to 18 May is celebrated with not less scope. St. Alexander's Day every year is marked with a beautiful procession, during which the inhabitants of the island wear dresses of various historical eras. The parade starts from the Aragonese castle, and ends at the church of St. Alexander.

On Easter there is "the run of the Angel", when the believers with the angel Gabriel on their shoulders run in the crowd. During the day of St. Anne opposite the Aragonese castle, there is a large-scale play organized in the sea. At the end of May, anyone in Ischia Ponte can witness the folk dance of La Naredzat. The ships were also involved during the three-day celebration of St. Michael Day in September. The gourmets should visit Andar per Cantine in September and taste the local products. In October, the Wine Festival takes place. If you like cinema, then come to Ischia in the summer to see the Festival of Cinema and the Ischia Global Award.

Where to stay?

Top-rated hotels

Best hotels for short vacation or business trip to Isola di Ischia
Miramare E Castello

Guests of Isola di Ischia can choose from over 200 of various hotels the island's capital; those include Miramare E Castello hotel. This luxurious hotel offers its guests magnificent rooms with panoramic view over Aragonese castle; it's an excellent choice for fans of beach rest. The hotel amazes with elegant decorations and there are items of past centuries everywhere around. Romantic resting area with jacuzzi is set up on the hotel's roof; gourmets are welcome at the restaurant with panoramic terrace.

Mare Blu Terme

Mare Blu Terme five-star hotel is situated in the very heart of the capital just a few steps away from the main shopping street of the island. It occupies an amazing old villa and features a huge swimming pool with thermal water. It's an excellent place for fascinating vacations, especially for those caring of their health. The hotel offers lots of extra healthcare services, including upscale day spa and a modern gym.

Mezzatorre

Well-known Mezzatorre hotel is situated in Forio town. It's quite popular among tourists preferring red-carpet vacations. The hotel features a large territory with swimming pools, sun terraces, excellent restaurants and bars. Despite its high profile, the hotel is known for its informal and homelike atmosphere. In the morning the hotel offers its guests a wide selection of home-made bakery, while seafood lovers will be impressed with menu of the restaurant. Mezzatorre also has several tennis courts and jogging tracks making it a good choice for sports fans.

Lieta

Beautiful Lieta villa is located next to Aragonese castle. It is aimed to those preferring romantic leisure. The lodge is situated on top of a small hill with an amazing panoramic view over the coastline. Hotel rooms are decorated in traditional style that deserves the highest praise. Rooms are furnished with elegant furniture and rich textiles and enriched with noble wood finishing. Lieta is an excellent place to take a break from daily routine.

Il Moresco

Il Moresco grand hotel is another interesting choice and a truly unique accommodation place. Its look resembles a formidable palace surrounded with a high lava stone wall. An amazing pine forest is located next to the hotel; it would take only a couple of minutes to get to the busy shopping street. The main advantage of Il Moresco is its large healthcare center with beautiful thermal pools and relaxation areas.

Continental TermeThe biggest thermal complex of the island can be found at the Continental Terme hotel featuring a large staff of world-class medics. This luxurious resort complex will suit the most demanding tourists. It offers excellent environment for family vacations.

Younger tourists will be delighted with bright kids club and numerous playgrounds.

Shopping in Isola di Ischia

Shopping in Isola di Ischia authentic goods, best outlets, malls and boutiques

Ischia is not the best place to buy brand clotheas from world famous designers. If you want to buy not Italian products, but any other brands, then you should better consider a trip to Naples. It won't take long, and the variety of choice of clothes, shoes, perfumes, and accessories in continental Italy is much greater than on the island. The locals themselves, for example, prefer to make large purchases there. Nevertheless, even on Ischia, you can find the quality of local production. You can also find imported products here, of course, but the prices are not the lowest.

The largest concentration of shops is on Via Roma in Ischia Port, which originates in the port. You can also find a large warehouse store in Florio. There is also an outlet on the island, though it is only one. Going shopping, keep in mind that local stores start working at 8.30 in the morning, work steadily until one in the afternoon, and then reopen only at 16.30. When the store closes for the night depends only on its owner in summer many shops are open almost until midnight. However, it is worth remembering that the Italians are not famous for punctuality, therefore the shop you liked may be closed even when, in theory, it should be open. Keep in mind that on Sunday and Monday morning almost everything is closed, and on Thursday, the work time is usually reduced.

Those, who watch after their skin and love everything natural, should take a closer look at the products of the local company Le Terme della Bellezza. The cosmetics made from natural components with the mandatory addition of local medicinal waters in one form or another is sold in most of the island's SPA centers. Local perfume Sapori d'Ischia is also interesting. Those who want to bring good clothes and shoes from Ischia should visit such brand stores as Brunello Cucinelli, YSL, Prada, Liu Jo, Stuart Weitzman, Fendi. The products of these firms are produced in Italy, therefore the prices for it are very pleasant.

If you want to buy goods for children in Ischia, then you should visit the store Cicco the commune of Barano. There is every chance of even getting a discount if you bargain well.

Also, children's goods stores, Io Bimbo and Universo Bimbo, are located in Casamicciola. By the way, they sell things not only for newborns and preschoolers but also for teenagers. Besides clothing and footwear, here you can find toys, hygiene products and household chemicals for children. The ceramic factory Melella, which is obligatory for visiting for every traveler, is located in the same area. For five centuries, they have been producing here various ceramic products, and anyone can become familiar with the technique of its production. The products from the factory you can buy right there for a small price for such a unique souvenir.

Be sure to buy at least one bottle of local wine for yourself or as a gift. Pietratorcia Vigne di Chignole, Perrazzo Bianco superior, Ischia

Bianco are made from grapes grown on the island. The liqueur will also be an excellent souvenir. Fortunately, the assortment of this drink is huge here: bright yellow Limoncello with lemon, in some ways, is a landmark of the island, Nocillo with nut, Rucolino with herbs, melon, strawberry, and orange for any taste and price. You can also buy local pasta, olive oil, balsamic vinegar, coffee, and cheese. Look closely at leather products from local craftsmen and jewelry. An original present to a loved one will be a carnival mask, which there are a lot here.

Things to See in Ischia

Ischia is the largest of Campania's islands, covering about 46 sq. km (18 sq. miles). Its velvety slopes, green with pine woods and vineyards, have earned it the nickname Isola Verde (Green Isle), while its fame as a healthy retreat has earned it another nickname, Island of Eternal Youth, for its peaceful atmosphere and its spas. These are fueled by the widespread volcanic activity still present on the island, although its volcano, Mount Epomeo, has long been dormant. Hot springs, mineral-water springs, and steam and hot-mud holes dot the island's slopes.

Once separate, Ischia Porto and Ischia Ponte have now merged into one; together they make up the largest town on the island, lying on its northeastern corner. The two are linked by the pleasant promenade of Via Roma and Corso Vittoria Colonna (known locally as "Il Corso") stretching about 2km (1 1/4 miles). The majority of activity is concentrated in Ischia

Porto, around its naturally round harbor which is, in fact, an extinct volcano crater. The town was founded in the 18th century by the Bourbons who fell in love with a villa-cum-spa built by a doctor, Francesco Buonocore, and decided to establish their residence there. They transformed the villa overlooking the lake into a small palace -what happened to the doctor is unknown; maybe he graciously donated his home to their majesties -the Casina Reale Borbonica, which today houses a military spa (closed to the public). They also cut a channel into the outer shore of the lake, transforming it into the present-day large harbor. Inaugurated in 1854, it has been the island's major port ever since. Today, Ischia Porto is a typically bustling and attractive Mediterranean port town with a yacht-filled marina, a busy commercial port, and plenty of restaurants and bars strung out along the water's edge.

Ischia Ponte is more attractive and retains something of the atmosphere of a sleepy fishing village. It is dominated by the vast bulk of the Castello Aragonese which looms over the town from atop a rocky islet that is linked to the main island by a causeway-like bridge (or "ponte"). This islet, with its small natural harbor, is the site of the original Greek settlement which was fortified in the 5th century B.C. Alfonso of Aragon re-inforced the fortifications in the mid-15th century and added the bridge. We recommend a visit to the castle (Piazzale Aragonese, Ischia Ponte, tel. 081-992834; 10€ adults, 6€ youth 9-19; free for children 8 and under; winter 10am-4:30pm, summer 9am-7:30pm) for the spectacular views from its terraces and ramparts; you can take the elevator to the top or walk up, but it's a steep climb. The last eruption of Mount Epomeo, in 1301, destroyed most of the village that had grown around the small natural harbor. The population resettled, but closer to the castle and bridge.

A short distance (6.5km/4 miles) from Ischia town, along the coast to the west, lies the small village of Casamicciola Terme, with its scenic harbor and marina (although, being right on the main road, its charm is compromised somewhat by the traffic), and Villa Ibsen, where the famous Norwegian writer wrote *Peer Gynt.* Founded in the 16th century to take advantage of the area's thermo-mineral springs, Casamicciola Terme is where the first "modern" spa was opened on the island in

1604. Tragedy struck, however, in 1883 when the village was virtually destroyed by a violent earthquake. It was immediately rebuilt, but closer to the shore, in its current position by the marina. The remains of the original town can be seen a little way inland in the hamlet of Bagni, with the island's oldest spas opening onto its main square, and in the village of Majo, farther up the slope.

Adjacent to Casamicciola, 8km (5 miles) west of Ischia Porto, is the picturesque Lacco Ameno, famous for the mushroom-shaped rock that stands in the shallow water a few yards from the sandy shore. The ancient Greeks established their first settlement on this coast, although daunted by the frequent -at that time -earthquakes and eruptions, they never developed a colony. An unassuming fishing harbor until the 1950s, it was then shaken out of its torpor by Italian publisher Angelo Rizzoli. He built his villa on the promontory of Monte Vico, overlooking the village to the west, and decided to invest in the area and transform it into an exclusive resort. His plan was successful and the promontory has become the most exclusive spa destination in Italy, offering many luxurious hotels and villas. Villa Arbusto, Angelo Rizzoli's own summer home, is today a museum -Museo Civico Archeologico di Pithecusae (tel. 081-900356; admission 3€; Tues-Sun 9:30am-1pm and 4-8pm) -displaying the findings of local archaeological excavation. It is worth a visit, if only to admire the famous Coppa di Nestore or Nestor's Cup. Dating from 725 B.C., this drinking vessel bears one of the oldest known Greek inscriptions, which, appropriately, celebrates the wine of Ischia. Nearby is an important Catholic pilgrimage site, the Sanctuary of Santa Restituta (tel. 081-980161; daily 10am-1pm and 4-7pm), with its attached archaeological excavations and museum. The original church was created in the 4th or 5th century A.D. by adapting an ancient Roman water cistern, and later restructured.

On the west side of the Monte Vico promontory are the lovely gardens of Villa La Mortella, Via F. Calise 39, 80075 Forio (tel. 081-986220). Covering 2 hectares (5 acres), the gardens were created by the famous British landscape gardener Russell Page for Susana Walton, the Argentinean wife of composer Sir William Walton, who collected many rare botanical species. Admission is 12€ for adults,

10€ for children 8 to 16 and adults over 60, 6€ for children 5 to 7, and free for children 4 and under (Apr 1-Nov 15 Tues, Thurs, and Sat-Sun 9am-7pm; ticket booth closes 30 min. earlier).

On the western coast of the island, 13km (8 miles) west of Ischia Porto, is the lively town of Forio, with its wealth of bars and beaches. Popular among Naples residents, it is usually bypassed by foreign tourists. A favorite retreat of writers and musicians for centuries, Forio is known for its plethora of fine restaurants and its particularly delicious locally produced wine. The attractive town centre is dominated by Il Torrione, a solid, late-15th-century watchtower that was one of 12 such constructions built to ward off frequent Saracen attacks. It is occasionally opened for special exhibitions. La Colombaia, Via F. Calise 130, 80075 Forio (tel.

081-3332147), is the historic villa of Italian film director Luchino Visconti; it houses a film school and a small museum (Mon-Sat 9:30am-12:30pm and 3:30-6:30pm). Our favorite church on Ischia, the tiny, whitewashed Madonna del Soccorso stands in a spectacular position on a headland jutting out to sea just to the west of the town. Inside, you will find model ships offered to the Madonna by sailors who have survived shipwrecks.

The southern half of Ischia is more agricultural, with only one town on the southern shore: the tiny fishing harbor of Sant'Angelo, 11km (7 miles) south of Ischia Porto. Shaded by a tall promontory jutting into the sea and connected to the shore by a sandy isthmus (10m-long/328 ft.) that is closed to vehicles, it is one of Ischia's most picturesque sights. Far from the hype of the high-priced spa resorts, it is quite exclusive and secluded. The other villages on this part of the island are nestled on the steep slopes of the mountain, overlooking the sea. Serrara Fontana (9.5km/6 miles southwest of Ischia Porto) is a tiny hamlet centered on a lookout terrace affording spectacular views.

Flower Power -Ischia's unusual volcanic characteristics have produced more than spa-perfect conditions. The fertile soil and unique subtropical climate have been so favorable to flowering plants and shrubs that you can find on the island 50% of the entire European patrimony of flower species, a number of them indigenous to Ischia.

Day Spas in Ischia

What attracts most visitors to Ischia are the island's many spas, which offer an endless variety of thermo-mineral health and beauty treatments. With over 56 different mineral springs scattered across the island's slopes and beaches, Ischia is spa-paradise with a natural resource that has been harnessed by over 150 spa operators.

A number of the island's modern facilities operate as day parks and are perfect for a one-off visit. If you want to stay longer, many hotels have their own spas and will offer package stays including meals and basic spa services, such as the use of the thermo-mineral pools. Even if you are not particularly interested in spa treatments, the outdoor spa parks are a unique and relaxing experience. *Note:* Many establishments specialize in medical treatments, in which even beauty care and stress relief are tackled from a scientific rather than a pampering viewpoint. In any case, remember to pack an old swimsuit, possibly dark colored, as the high mineral content of some waters will stain the fabric, or leave a sulfurous smell that is almost impossible to remove.

Located between Ischia Porto and Casamicciola, Parco Termale Castiglione (tel. 081-982551), is a state-of-the-art facility offering thermo-mineral waters and mud treatments in a mix of indoor and open-air facilities. The scenic outdoor pools range in temperature from 82° to 104°F (28°-40°C). On the promontory of Monte Vico near Lacco Ameno, you'll find Parco Termale Negombo (tel. 081-986152), nestled in the island's most picturesque cove, Lido di San Montano. Here you can enjoy magnificent gardens, a secluded beach, and elegant thermal pools. South of Forio, on the pretty Bay of Citara, is Parco Termale Giardini Poseidon, Via Giovanni Mazzella Citara, Forio d'Ischia (tel. 081-9087111), an open-air facility with 22 pools (both relaxing and curative), a large private beach, and several restaurants. Finally, to the east of Sant'Angelo, you'll find the Parco Termale Giardini Aphrodite-Apollon (tel. 081-999219), an indoor-outdoor facility with lovely grounds and pools that is part of the Park Hotel Miramare.

For a more traditional spa experience, we recommend the state-of-the-art Ischia Thermal Center, Via delle Terme 15, Ischia (tel. 081-984376), which offers a wide range of health and beauty treatments. We also recommend the four historical spas of Casamicciola Terme - Terme Manzi, Belliazzi, Elisabetta, and Lucibello -that open onto the famous Piazza Bagni in the hamlet of Bagni. For an even more exclusive experience, head to the Terme della Regina Isabella, a five-star hotel and thermal resort in Lacco Ameno and one of the most elegant spas on the island.

Best Nightlife in Ischia

The sweet Ischitan nights are best spent outdoors, enjoying a bit of people-watching from the terraces of the many cafes strategically located on the most picturesque seaside promenades and panoramic outlooks. The elegant cafes around the harbor in Ischia are perfect for *aperitivo,* but we also like the unassuming Da Lilly, a shack on the rocks, with a simple terrace overlooking the Spiaggia dei Pescatori in Ischia Ponte. La Floreana (tel. 081-999570), at the belvedere of Serrara Fontana, is perfect for a sunset *aperitivo* (there is also a simple restaurant).

Another great place for a sundowner (plus dinner if you like) is the laid-back La Tavernetta del Pirata (tel. 081-999251), which overlooks the little harbor at Sant'Angelo. Other pleasant cafes line the seaside promenade of Forio and Lacco Ameno; we enjoy Bar Franco, Via Roma 94, Lacco Ameno (tel. 081-980880), where you can sit at the pleasant outdoor terrace facing the beach or simply sample their excellent ice cream. We are rather partial to ice cream and highly recommend those made at De Maio, Piazza Antica Reggia 9, Ischia Porto (tel. 081-

991870), the best ice-cream parlor on the island; claiming 80 years of experience, the shop makes wonderful creamy flavors. A few doors away is Da Ciccio, Via Porto 1, Ischia Porto (no phone), which makes more creative flavors by adding in nuts, chocolate bits, and so on.

We recommend the concerts of classical music and jazz organized by the William Walton Foundation in the lovely gardens of Villa La Mortella, Via F. Calise no. 35, 80075 Forio Isola d'Ischia (tel. 081-986220). The season runs from April to November; concert tickets include admission to the garden and cost 20€ for adults, 15€ for children 13 to 18, and 10€ for children 6 to 12. If you are lucky enough to be on the island for the Ischia Jazz Festival in September, make advance reservations for the scheduled concerts, which usually include some famous international names.

Active Pursuits in Ischia

Ischia's shoreline alternates between rugged cliffs and stretches of sand, to the delight of sunbathers and swimmers. The island's beautiful beaches are all the more special because they are a commodity almost completely lacking in the Bay of Naples and the Amalfi Coast. The town of Ischia has a beach - or rather several small ones, the best being the Spiaggia dei Pescatori, where local fishermen beach their boats, a short distance west of the Aragonese Castle. You can do way better, though. The island's most beautiful beach is Spiaggia dei Maronti, stretching for about 2km (1 1/4 miles) east of the village of Sant'Angelo, straight down the cliff from Barano d'Ischia (4km/2 1/2 miles south of Ischia Porto), but be warned; like others on the island, these long, scenic stretches of sand are very crowded in the summer. The Spiaggia di Cartaromana, down from the village of San Michele on the east coast of the island, is on a slightly more secluded cove. North of Forio is the Spiaggia di San Francesco, overlooked by the promontory of Monte Vico, while south of Forio is the Spiaggia di Citara, which used to be the island's largest and most beautiful sandy beach. Though much diminished by erosion, it is still very pleasant and is popular for the hot mineral springs that flow out to sea at its southern edge; these springs are the same ones that are used by the spa Giardini Poseidon. We also highly recommend renting a boat from one of the harbors and visiting the many coves that are accessible only by sea.

If you are not into swimming or relaxation, you can leave the shoreline and explore the island's hinterland which is dotted with vineyards producing excellent D.O.C. wines. You could combine wine tasting with some interesting hikes up the slopes of Mount Epomeo. We recommend you get hold of a copy of the small brochure from the tourist office in Ischia, titled *Lizard Trails,* which has descriptions and maps of the island's best trails.

Explore Nearby Towns

Isola di Vivara

The deserted island of Vivara is like something in a movie. Uninhabited, wild, and rising from the deep blue sea, it looks like the set for a thriller film. The crescent-shaped crater was once a volcano and is part of a chain of little islands in the Gulf of Naples. It is connected to bigger, more famous Procida by a long strip of footbridge.

Vivara is a nature preserve left entirely in its natural state. It is covered with local Mediterranean climate fauna, including six rare orchid species, primrose and an abundance of ferns. It hosts migratory birds and is a nature lover's paradise to explore. The woods were once the hunting grounds of King Charles III of Napoli who used it in pursuit of pheasant and rabbit. (Maybe that's how rabbit became the staple dish of Ischia? Hmm, to ponder!)

Cross from Procida to Vivara on the bridge and pass into a natural realm of undisturbed environmental wonders.

Casamicciola Terme

Casamicciola Terme lounges on the northern shore of the island of Ischia. With about 8000 inhabitants, the town enjoys a lively isle atmosphere that expands greatly in the summer.

Originally named "Casa Nizzola" (Nizzola's home) , the city's coat of arms portrays the old lady NIzzola with her feet immersed in the town's famous hot springs, with are said to cure any ailment. It symbolizes the thermal waters that made Cassamicciola, and Ischia in general, famous. In ancient times, the locals used to bake clay pots and other pottery on the natural heat emitted from the rocks. The same heat was exploited for cooking and other housework. At the lovely restaurant "Il Castiglione" archeologists found some traces of an ancient village dating back to the Iron Age. The island hosts the osservatorio geofisico, with one of the earliest earthquake measurement devices.

While Casamicciola Terme is a port town and the main settlement is along the waterfront, you'll also be stunned by some natural marvels, like the extinct volcano, Vulcano Rotaro, and the height of Mt. Epomeo that rises to 780 meters above sea level. There are chestnut and pine woods beyond the town, as well. Trails and roads lead to villages in the hills, where you can enjoy some time in nature away from the crowds.

Just below the hill of Castiglione, the gorgeous turquoise sea is embellished by the Grotto of Sibilla. Legend holds that Sibilla Cumana was a prophetess who foresaw the future. She used to live in Cuma, an old village on the mainland near Naples. When the king Aristodemo ascended the throne of Cuma, Sibilla was constantly beckoned and bothered from the king himself. One day Sibilla, in order to demonstrate her power and how much she held the king in contempt, called her Vestals to lie on the sea over a huge mantle. She suddenly got on the mantle and, under the astonished eyes of the king and his courtiers, departed towards Ischia and took up her residence into the Grotto of Castiglione, later called "Grotto of Sibilla".

Casamicciola was home to the most popular thermal spas in all of Campania. This historic spa was established in 1610 and was popular with Neapolitan nobles, and even Garibaldi came to rest in the curative waters. Later, the king expanded it in order to allow anybody to enjoy the amazing benefits of those natural thermal springs. Taking advantages of the free board, lodging and cures, every poor person of the island had the possibility to enjoy Casamicciola for 2 entire weeks per year. The resort was originally based in the area of Piazza dei Bagni and benefited the natural spring of Gurgitiello but, after the disastrous earthquake of 1883, it was rebuilt on the seashore.

Today, Casamicciola is home to a couple of immense thermal parks, that are part garden and part thermal spas, with various pools and tubs, along with a menu of treatment options, such as facials, massages, and more. The most noted are Castiglione and O'Vagnitiello. Castiglione is a complex with ten separate pools of various temperatures that are said to help cure arthritis and other muscle aches, along with mud wraps and hydrotherapy. Its unique feature is the panoramic funicular that transports guests from the entrance to the pool area. O'Vignitiello is a tropical garden with four pools amidst the plants and sea views. Another noted spa is the five-star upscale Manzi Resort, a high level luxury hotel and spa complex done up with Moorish flair.

In Casamicciola you can browse the shops and stop in at Bar Calise for a coffee, pastry, drink or snack. The well-noted restaurant U'Guarracino is in Casamicciola, at the

Castiglione Thermal Park. It is one of Ischia's most famous restaurants, and definitely worth a meal here!

The beach at the Marina is a soft sandy stretch that is easily accessible, right in town.

Discover attractions in Casamicciola Terme

Barano d'Ischia

Barano is Ischia's second largest town and one that has kept its painstakingly planted and tended vineyards and vegetable gardens. In fact, the island's wines have been heralded at home and abroad. Try the *Biancolella* and the *Per 'e Palummo* for flavours you will never forget.

The very fertile land of this stunning volcanic place attracted many colonizers. The Greeks built a notable nymphaeum, under the warm protection of the nymphs Nitrodi and Apollo, protector of beauty and health. The artifacts found there are currently preserved into the National Archeology Museum in Naples. There are still traces of the Greek and Roman origins in some expressions of the local dialect deriving from those ancient languages.

Barano d'Ischia unfolds over the rolling hills that give way to the southern seaside of the island, interlacing the *macchia*, breathtaking wooded craters and mountains. The territory is divided into several hamlets under the municipality of Barano, scattered around the delightful hills. The hamlets have rich history and traditions lost in time. The population has peasant origins.

The main magnet for tourists is the bay of Maronti, a splendid natural bay that is two kilometers long, with fabulous beaches and evocative areas, such as the valleys of Cava Scura and Ormitello, reachable from Buonapane.

You will be impressed from the spacious solemnity of the central piazza, and the historical center flows off of the piazza, where you will admire ancient buildings dating to XVIII and XIX centuries in all their pure austere elegance.

The most important thermal spring is Nitrodi, a thermal park and garden that is popular for the high quality if the curative waters and the spa treatments offered.

Discover attractions in Barano d'Ischia

Serrara Fontana

The island of Ischia never fails to surprise. It offers an endless series of breathtaking views and gorgeous scenery. This is certainly the case of Serrara Fontana, whose appeal is both mountain and seaside. The town of Serrara Fontana itself is the highest village on the island, at 360 meters above sea level. Its perch on the ridge-top offers spectacular panoramic views. Wander to the town's belvedere, a communal balcony that overlooks the landscape. Lesser known is the piazzetta, which offers great vistas of the Gulf of Naples with the islands of Procida and Vivara.

From the Piazzetta you can walk the old mule path that leads to the peak of Mt. Epomeo, where you'll find the little church dedicated to St. Nicholas and its accompanying hermitage.

The municipality of Serrara Fontana includes a couple of outlying villages, the most interesting of which is the fishing village of Sant'Angelo. A pedestrian town that fronts the sea, it is a charming place full of character and color. The beach of Le Fumarole is a fascinating place to visit it boasts the strange phenomenon of sand that emits volcanic vapors! The heat is said to be curative. The ancient volcanic activity also provides a series of hot springs around the island. Visit the "thermal parks" between Sant'Angelo and Maronti, where you can enjoy hot natural spring pools, hydromassage, and a plethora of luxuriant spa treatments.

Discover attractions in Serrara Fontana

Sant'Angelo di Ischia

A captivating town on the island of Ischia, Sant'Angelo is worth visiting. The old fishing village retains tons of charm in its narrow streets that are lined with white-washed and pastel painted buildings. Terraces and balconies offer fabulous views of the marina and sea. The village follows the crescent shape of the coast and has good beaches and quiet coves for swimming and sunbathing.

Sant'Angelo has long been the haunt of artists and intellectuals. The heart of Sant'Angelo is the Piazzetta, a lively central square that opens to the beach for the sun worshippers, while showcasing boutiques, art galleries, shops, bars and restaurants for shopping and fun, both day and night. Many of our guests tell us that they found great souvenirs and interesting items to take home here.

The volcanic origins of the island have enriched it with abundant thermal springs, making it a popular destination for spa goers. At Cava Petrelle you'll find the famous "fumarole" weird heat vapors that emit through the sand! Cavascura offers a thermal playground in the natural rocks, caves and waterfalls. There are plenty of spas for those who want massage, facial and other treatments.

Sant'Angelo's biggest party is the annual Festa di San Michele, where the statue of the saint is carried through the streets of the town before then going for a boat ride. It's followed by a concert in the piazza and fireworks.

Ferries transport you to Ischia, and buses will get you to the village of Sant'Angelo.

Forio d'Ischia

Forio is a picture-perfect town, perfectly framed in its seting between the colourful landscapes of Mount Epomeo and the crystalline sea. It is the most populated town on the Isle of Ischia. Its pretty boat marina, white sand beaches, and pastel buildings make it alluring.

The roots of the name is under debate: some say it derives from a dialectal expression that someone, fed up with the overcrowding at the castle Aragonese, decided to "get out" (*forio*) of there; while some historians say it derives from the classic language, meaning fertile or land of flowers. Whatever origins, Forio is one of the most fascinating places of the island for the spectacular multi-hued beauty of the landscapes and architectural richness.

The Church of St Maria del Soccorso (XVI century) characterized by different styles including Moorish, and is located onto the promontory hanging over the sea on the cliff. That magical point offers stunning sunsets and lovely views of the towers, built in the XVI century and used as defensive look-outs against Saracen pirates. Among them, the majestic "Torrione" stands out, a cylindrical structure placed at the center of the town.

The stunning villas built on the rocky promontory around Punta Caruso will surely catch your eye. The highlight is the beautiful former residence of a popular English composer, Sir William Walton; the estate known as La Mortella has been turned into a breathtaking garden. The different climate zones show off more than 800 rare and beautiful plants, and it has been named among the most beautiful gardens in Italy. The eye-popping panoramas alone are worth the visit, but the garden really is something special.

One of the most enchanting beaches in Forio is Citara, rich in thermal springs; the name derives from an ancient temple dedicated to the goddess Venus Citara, now a temple of a different kind a thermal park dedicated to wellness called Giardini Poseidon. It is the biggest thermal park of Ischia, with manicured gardens and a private beach. Good restaurants, a "grotto" digged into the rock , shops, a newsstand and a bar guarantee a perfect stay. Enjoy lovely walk through the fantastic flowered beds and stunning baths with different temperatures.

Panza, extremely pretty hamlet of Forio, so appreciated by the Germans and tranquillity seekers. The typical landascape is characterized by the vulcanic crater of Campotese, where to find incredible vineyards and restaurants to taste the wine and local food.

The most important wine house in Ischia is called "D'Ambra Vini" and is located in Panza, where you'll have the possibility to visit the museum of the folk wisdom of the isle, "Museo del contadino".

If you rather are in the mood to try a totally new free experience, go to Sorgeto bay. Here a thermal spring heats the seawater and you can easily enjoy a bath all over the year, in natural pools formed by rounded stones.

Discover attractions in Forio d'Ischia

Lacco Ameno

Lacco Ameno on Ischia is known for its giant mushroom that juts from the sea. While there are many legends about lovers and gods to explain the unique formation, the tufa rock called Il Fungo is the result of the volcanic activity that blessed the island with its hot mineral springs.

The town itself gets its name from the tufa stone: The Greek word lakkos means "rock". After the unification of Italy the municipality decided to embellish it a bit and added Ameno (Greek for pleasant). The result is indeed a pleasant place with a vibrant mix of rustic and upscale blending together. Lacco Ameno faces the beautiful Bay of Montano where rocky hills plunge into the sea and add interest to the landscapes. The nice shoreline offers both reefs and beaches, and boats bob happily in the bay.

Lacco Ameno is the smallest of the towns on Ischia. Its tree-lined streets and deluxe shops are attractive, accentuated by white houses, little churches and old palazzi facing the sea. Behind on Monte Vico is the Torre Aragonese tower that once watched for Saracen invasions, still standing guard. The main church is dedicated to the town's patron saint Santa Restituta and there is a museum attached to it. An archeological area Pithecusae displays the area's ancient origins.

Every May 16 Lacco Ameno pays homage to their patron saint with a grand festa in her honor. The "virgin saint" Santa Restituta was martyred in northern Africa and her body put on a boat, which was set aflame and put out to sea. The fire didn't consume her and the boat was guided ashore here "by the wings of angels" and her martyred body buried, and the church built in her name. The festa takes the statue of Santa Restituta aboard a boat for a benediction of the mariners. It is also the occasion to recall the sacking by the Turks in the early 1600s. They entered the church, knocked down the statue of the saint with a great scimitar and stole the bells from the tower. They loaded them in the boats and took off, but a storm came up and they were forced to throw the bells overboard to avoid sinking. The local fishermen dredged them out of the water and the storm immediately calmed.

Quick Guide for New Travelers

Ischia is the largest island in the bay of Naples and is considered by many to be the most beautiful, (though Capri is considerably more famous). The island is 10 km from east to west and 7 km north to south. It has a coastline of 34 km and covers an area of 46.3 sq km. It has a permanent population of approximately 58,000. Up to 6 million tourists (principally from the Italian mainland and Germany) flock to the island for its volcanic thermal spas and as well for its beaches and food.

Cities

Several towns are located along the island's coast. The largest city in Ischia is actually (and often confusingly, for tourists) called Ischia. The town of Ischia, however, has two different centers: Ischia Porto and Ischia Ponte. Ischia Porto is the commercial center of the island

and is named after the main port. Ischia Ponte ("ponte" meaning "bridge" in Italian) is named for the area surrounding and including the footbridge that was constructed to connect the Castello Aragonese with the island. Beside the town of Ischia, some of the other centres are Lacco Ameno, Casamicciola, Forio, Barano, Sant'Angelo, and the jointed town of Serrara-Fontana.

- ✓ Barano
- ✓ Casamicciola
- ✓ Forio
- ✓ Ischia Ponte
- ✓ Ischia Porto
- ✓ Lacco Ameno
- ✓ Serrara-Fontana

Other destinations

✓ Sant'Angelo

Understand

Ischia — historically called *Pitecusae* — has been colonized in turn by the Greeks, Syrausansa, Romans, Saracens, Turks, and Aragonese; all of whom were interested in its excellent strategic position as well as its therapeutic hot-spring waters and of course its attractive landscape. The result of all this varied history can be seen in the ruins of various outposts, towers, and "*tufa*" rock shelters hidden all over the island.

More recently Ischia has become a frequent backdrop for Italian and American movies such as *"Vacanze ad Ischia"*, *"Appuntamento ad Ischia"*, and *"The Talented Mr.Ripley"*. The island has also been used as a cinematic stand-in for the Island of Capri.

Climate

The best time for the traveler to visit Ischia is from April to October, however, the weather in Ischia is always changing and visitors should expect both sunshine and rain — whatever the season. Summer, the main tourist season, combines long, hot days with lengthy evenings. Winter can be bitterly cold and wet, with short daylight hours.

Flora and fauna

Also called the *"Green Island"*, Ischia enjoys hot and dry summers and mild winters along with a pronounced fertility which is a result of having almost an entirely volcanic soil. These factors allow Mediterranean plants to thrive all over the island, and sub-tropical and tropical species to successfully occupy niches in the warmest areas.

On the Southern side of the island, the continuous exposure to direct sunlight favors tropical and desert vegetation which is mainly represented by palms, cactus' and agave plants with Mediterranean trees hiding in the shade of inlets and bends. On the Northern side of the island in the shade cast by Mount Epomeo, you'll find chestnut trees, as well as typical Mediterranean trees such as the holm oak, cypress, and cork trees as well as cultivated almond trees, vines, and olive trees.

Ischia Mud

Ischia mud originates from the geologic evolution of the island where, over the centuries, many hydrovolcanic eruptions and earthquakes changed the soil composition. The hot waters and muds, all *"thermal"* or *"hypertermal"* i.e. they are at the same time hot or very hot and very rich in minerals content. In spite of their diversity, all the muds have the same standard features: sodium, chlorine, potassium, calcium and sulphur in the form of sulphates and sulphides. Because of the variety of different chemicals found in them, different waters and mud are recommended for *different treatments*. The Italian Ministry of Health produces a document that has updates on which waters and muds are suitable for therapeutic treatments and illness and diseases which can be treated. According to this document, disease which can be treated are: rheumatic diseases such as arthrosis; respiratory diseases; dermatological diseases such as psoriasis, atopical dermatitis, eczema (except for exudative bladdery forms),

chronic seborrhea; gynecological diseases such as pelvis tissue sclerosis; diseases of the gastroenteric apparatus such as gastroenteric or bilious dyspepsia, and intestinal disorders associated with constipation.

Cavascura and Olmitello Thermal water

While traveling around Sant'Angelo there are several footpaths that can take you up the hilltops. One of these is a footpath that goes to the thermal springs of Cavascura and Olmitello. To get there, take a taxi boat from the square of Sant'Angelo to the Fumarole beach. Here, with the beach behind you, take the footpath from the right side of the beach which is flanked by oleander trees. The first stretch is steep, with a few houses on both sides, then it levels out and there are Mediterranean bushes and a variety of plants such as figs, capers, prickly pears, etc. On the right, there is a view of the Maronti beach. Passing under a natural arch, turn right to reach the beach. Here is the entrance to Cavascura. There are all types of typical restaurants and at the back of the canyon are the antique thermal springs of Cavascura. Going back, climbing the steps through the vine yards, you will arrive at the antique establishment of Cava Olmitello, which sadly to say is in disuse. Here, as you make your way through the bushes, with only the croaking of frogs, you can imagine yourself traveling back in time when the world was a much simpler place.

Talk
While Italian and Neapolitan are the native languages on the island, most people working

in the tourism industry speak at least one other language, with German and English being the most widely spoken second languages. It should also be noted that the island of Ischia also has its own dialect of Italian, which can make it difficult for visitors to understand at times.

Get in

By plane
There is no airport on the island. The closest airport is the Naples International Airport . it is possible by taxi to reach two harbours (*Beverello* and *Mergellina*) of Naples in 20-30 minutes although there is a fixed price to get to Beverello, making it the preferred choice. There is also the Alibus line, which connects directly with the harbour of Napoli Beverello.

From these harbours, regular ferry crossings connect to Ischia.

Budget Airlines

Reaching Ischia on the cheap is possible with the following budget airlines that fly to Naples and/or Rome airports:

EasyJet	Ryanair	German Wings
TuiFly.com	Vueling	Myair
SpainAir	TrawelFly	AirOne
Lufthansa	Transavia	Vueling
Brussels Airlines	BlueAir	Wizzair
Aer Lingus	Iberia	Smartwings
Seven Air	Austrian	

By car

From Rome (A1) From Bari (A16) From Salerno (A30). It is better to follow the road markings for the *Tangenziale* (bypass) (exit No. 12) and to go on towards Pozzuoli. Then go out at the Via Campana (exit No. 12) and go on towards the Harbour of Pozzuoli (ferries only), which is about four km far away. You can also reach the harbour of Naples Beverello (both ferries and hydrofoils). You *don't have to* turn into the *Tangenziale*, but to follow the road markings for the *Zona Portuale* (Harbour area) and, after the exit, to go on for the harbour, which is about five km far from the highway.

By train

There are no trains to Ischia. However, there are four railway stations that are close to one of the harbours of Naples/Pozzuoli:

✓ Naples Campi Flegrei. From this station it is easy to reach the harbor of Mergellina by taxi, bus, tram or underground. Mergellina is approximately 3 km away from the railway station.

✓ Naples Mergellina. This station is more or less 200 m far from the harbor of Mergellina.

✓ Naples Centrale or Naples Piazza Garibaldi. Both stations enable you to have an immediate access to Piazza Garibaldi, which is located around 4 km from the harbour of Naples Beverello and easily reachable by taxi, tram or bus.

✓ Pozzuoli The Cumana railline operates from Montesanto in Naples and follows the coastline for approximately 20 km before ending in Torregaveta (Bacoli). To reach the Pozzuoli harbour you get off at the stop for Pozzuoli. The harbour is five minute walk away.

By boat

Alilauro Hidrofoil
✓ From Naples Beverello to Forio

08:00 (to Alilauro) (weekdays) 09:35 (to Alilauro) (except Saturdays via Ischia) 10:30 (to Alilauro) (via Ischia) 14:35 (to Alilauro) 17:00 (To Alilauro)

Most boats arriving in Ischia stop first in Ischia Porto, and then make additional stops in Casamicciola and Forio.

✓ Pozzuoli Harbour. You can also reach Ischia by taking the ferry from the main harbour in Pozzuoli (and Procida).

Tips

Taxis in Naples to the boats:

It is easy to take a taxi from the rail station or airport to the harbour. In this case take a look at the *"Fix prices table"* that any taxi driver must show in his car. Taxi drivers will often try to get tourists to pay more than necessary for the short ride from central station to the port, so be sure to either bargain or ask for the fixed price (*prezzo fisso*). For example, from the rail station Centrale to the Beverello harbour the fix total price is currently 9.50 EUR total, not per person, nothing more (though they may not allow more than four people in a taxi at a time). From the airport to the harbour of Beverello the fix total price is currently 16 Euros.

Getting off the boat in Ischia:

When taking many of the ferries from Naples to Ischia, it is important to pay close attention when disembarking. Many people make the mistake of getting off the boat, and disembark at the island of Procida instead of Ischia. It is recommended that visitors ask the people working on the boat if the boat stops at Procida. Also, be sure to pay attention to which port you get off at, even if you are at the island of Ischia.

The ferry from Pozzuoli goes direct to Ischia Porto.

As stated above, different boats make stops at several ports. It is best to know exactly which town you are aiming for. If you do not have a specific city in mind, the largest hub of activity and the largest port is called "Ischia Porto" (this port city is often called simply "Ischia", although this can be confusing as it is also the name of the island as a whole). You can find transportation to other parts of the island, tourist information, and food and shelter there, if all else fails.

Get around

By bus
The public bus service connects the various urban centres of the island through frequent journeys, most of them having their terminus in the town of Ischia Porto close to the harbour. The fare for a single journey (valid 90 minutes) is € 1.20, with tickets purchasable in advance from newsstands, bars, travel agencies and tobacconists. Tickets can also be purchased on board from the driver (or sometimes a helper in the front of the bus who also shouts

out stop names) for the slightly higher price of € 1.70. Tickets valid for longer durations (for example one or two-day tickets) are also available, usually only from the official ticket centres like in Ischia Porto bus stop. All tickets must be validated on boarding the bus. Tickets are regularly checked. The busses are often very crowded. The bus stops are often near a very busy street with high traffic.

Two most important bus routes are called CD and CS, both of which starts from Ischia porto, takes a circular tour around the island, and returns again to Ischia porto. Bus CD takes a clockwise route, while CS takes a anti-clockwise route. Using one of these two buses, one can get a cheap and easy trip around the island (little over 1 hour total round trip time).

By taxi

As with many other tourist destinations, visitors should confirm the price to their destination with the taxi driver before getting into the taxi. With most taxis not running on a meter, this is the surest way to ensure that you are not overcharged. When taking an ad-hoc taxi (taxi drivers just hanging out on the street) it's also worth haggling about the price of the trip beforehand as usually the initially quoted price is higher than the normal price of the trip.

Sightseeing Tour

There are half-day roundtrips to all six communities of Ischia with stops at the most beautiful sightseeing stops of the islands. Price is €11.00.

<u>See</u>

Villas, Parks and Museums

✓ Villa La Colombaia (Forio) The Villa, which is surrounded by a superb park, was the residence of the movie director Luchino Visconti. It is now the seat of an cultural Institution dedicated to Visconti, which is involved in promoting cultural activities such as music, cinema, theatre, art exhibitions, work-shops, and cinema reviews. There is a museum dedicated to Luchino Visconti as well. The Villa and the the Park are accessible to public visits.

✓ Villa La Mortella (Forio San Francesco)

This park is located at Forio d'Ischia and was originally the property of the English composer William Walton, who lived in the Villa next door with his Argentinian wife, Susanna. The composer, arrived on the island in 1946, planting wonderful tropical and Mediterranean plants, some of which have now reached amazing proportions.

✓ Giardini Ravino (Forio Citara Bay) Botanical Garden with one of the richest collection of cacti and succulents cultivated outdoors in Europe. The garden, along with the mature areas around Villa Ravino, is the result of 50 years of great passion and loving work of Captain Giuseppe d'Ambra, the owner of the Villa. The exotic trees include palms, olive, lemon and orange, surprising scenery and rare and precious botanical specimens. Giardini Ravino is located atForio d'Ischia. A rich collection of cacti and succulents cultivated outdoors, constantly enriched with new species from all over the world and embellished with the extraordinary presents of the Woolemi Pine, the most sensational discovery of the century. .

✓ The Castle Castello Aragonese (Ischia Ponte) Is one of the most striking monuments on the island. It stands on a small island near Ischia Ponte and is reached by crossing a stone bridge. The castle is about 113 meters high and the climb can be made on an old mule track or by using a modern elevator that was installed in the seventies. The castle was built in 1441 by Alfonso D'Aragona on top of the ruins of an old fort that dated back to 474 B.C. This fortified castle was used to protect Ischia's population from pirate attacks. One of the exhibits in the castle is dedicated to various forms of medieval torture.

✓ Guevara Tower Ischia Ponte The tower represents as well as Castello Aragonese one of the best known symbols of the island. It is called Guevara or Michelangelo's Tower and is located in front of the Castle, and is surrounded by a lawn and facing the Sant'Anna rocks. The tower was rebuilt over the ruins of an earlier ancient fortress: it is likely one of the defence towers built from the 15th century to protect the Castle and the coast against enemy attacks. The tower derives its name from the Dukes of Guevara who were the owners since 1800. Its second name derives from a legend that

Michelangelo, who was a friend of the poet Vittoria Colonna, stayed in the tower when he was visiting the island. The tower is nowadays used as arts exhibition centre.

✓ Il Torrione Forio Since at least the 9th century many towers were constructed along Ischia coastline to provide warning and to defend the island from raids by pirates. One of those tower, called "Torrione" still exists. This tower is located in Forio, near the harbour. It was built in 1480, and has two floors: the ground floor has no access from outside and was used as for storing weapons and munitions, and a rain-water tank; on the upper floor, there was accommodation for the garrison (about 10 people) led by a "torriere" that had the task of quickly sighting of any enemy ships and sounding the alarm. On the top, there was a terrace provided for four cannons. Historians notice that many similar towers were built in Forio until the 18th century, however although many of them were now used as private residences of noble families. Sixteen similar fortresses have been counted between 1480 and 1700, plus five more towers built in the district of Panza, some with a squared base and others with a circular base. Many of these towers are still standing and are mainly private residences. The "Torrione", after it had been restored, became a municipal Museum (on the lower floor) while the upper floor was the home of the artist Giovanni Maltese from Forio and is now an art gallery hosting his pictures and sculptures collection.

✓ A. Rizzoli Museum The Angelo Rizzoli Museum is located in Villa Arbusto and contains a picture gallery about Angelo Rizzoli's stay on the island. He used to stay in Lacco Ameno where he promoted the restructuring of the ancient Santa Restituta baths and sponsored the construction of a series of large luxury hotels which in the 50's and 60's were the much loved destination for cinema stars and international jet-setters.

✓ Pithecusae Museum Lacco Ameno The Pithecusae Archaeological Museum is located at the main building of Villa Arbusto, in Lacco Ameno. The Villa was built in 1785 by Don Carlo Acquaviva,

Duke of Atri, in the same place where a farm called "dell'arbusto" ("arbusto" means " shrub" , in this case the reference is to a particular plant growing in the garden surrounding the building) existed. Over the years the Villa had many owners, until 1952, when it was purchased by the publisher and movie producer Angelo Rizzoli who sponsored the reconstruction of the ancient thermal bath, the construction of some large hotels and the restoration of Piazza Restituta in Lacco Ameno's main piazza. Villa Arbusto also has a splendid public garden. The museum houses many archaeological exhibits dating from the Prehistory to the Roman era. On the ground floor there is also a geological section, which explains how the

Ischia (Isola d'Ischia) Island Tourism Italy

presence of the volcanoes affected life on the island.

✓ The Soccorso's church Forio This church is devoted to "Santa Maria della neve" (Saint Maria of the snow), and was built on a steep promontory from which it takes its name. As with the "Torrione" tower, it is the symbol of the town of Forio and it is one of the most original architectural structures on the island. The Soccorso was founded as an Augustinian convent in about 1350 but it was suppressed in 1653, with its present form going back to 1864. The church is accessible by 20 steps of piperno, which leads to a small atrium with five crosses of pipernio. This church is world famous not only for its location but also for its singular facade, which is white and adorned by precious 700 majolicas representing saints and scenes of the Passion of Christ. The Soccorso's style is very original, it reassumes some architectures as Greek-Byzantine, Moorish and Mediterranian in harmonic shapes. The inside is very interesting because of the many types of volta. In the left chapel there is a thaumaturgical cross, a sculpture of Catalan inspiration, surely made on the 16th century. Close to this cross there are two marble medals, that were found in a medieval sarcophagus that was found in the castel of the antique cathedral of Ischia. This church retains various artifacts such as a shovel made by Cesare Calise that represents Saint Augustine, and a small basin of pipernio dated from the 9-

10th century. On 05 May 2002, during his Pastoral Visit, Pope John Paul II met with many young people in a square adjacent to the church of Our Lady Help of Christians.

Thermal Springs

Ischias thermal springs have been renowned since ancient times and have been tested by many Italian and foreign scientists, for their therapeutic features. Not only are the thermal waters used in baths and thermal gardens, but they can found in small springs on some beaches and streams of spouting that feature hot water gushing into the sea as well as steam spouts (fumaroles) with gases gushing from cracks in the soil. Fumaroles can also be observed on the slopes of the Mount Epomeo, particularly on cold days, or are located into small caves, called "stoves", and idiomatically "sudatori" or "sudaturi" (from the Italian verb meaning "to perspire") which are used as a kind of sauna in baths and thermal gardens.

Springs and spouting steam can be considered as the manifest sign of Ischia's volcanic origins and of the still persisting volcanic activity. The particular features of the subsoil, due to its structure and chemical composition affect the minerals content and the degree of dilution by sea and rain water. According to many scientists, the location and features of the springs are affected by the combination of the above mentioned factors. The most ancient springs are those of Casamicciola, consecrated to the god Apollo, those of Lacco Ameno consacrated to Hercules, those of Citara in

Panza consacrated to Venus Citarea, and those of Barano consacrated to Nitrodi Nymps.

Churches

As described above, there is a tiny white-washed church located in a truly spectacular position: in the square on the Punta del Soccorso in Forio, that looks out onto the crystal clear sea a typically Mediterranean site of astounding beauty.

Do

Beaches
- ✓ Chiaia Forio: the perfect beach for children;
- ✓ Cava dell'Isola: Forio, the most important beach for young people;

- ✓ Citara Panza: This beach is at the foot of Epomeo, and is one of the most popular on the island. The crystal-clear water that laps the beach mixes with the thermal water spas in several points, allowing you to bathe in the sea and reap the benefit of thermal water at the same time. However, much of this beach is privately owned and the public areas are small and often overcrowded. In this bay there is also the Poseidon Thermal Garden;

- ✓ Bay of Saint Montano: Lacco Ameno. Is a bay where the thermal park Negombo is located. This unusual beach, located between Mount Vico and Mount Zaro, is unique compared to the island's other beaches. The clear sea water is very hot and the water is extremely shallow;

✓ Cartaromana: Ischia Ponte. This beach is located between Castello Aragonese and the Sant'Anna cliffs. The beach also offers one of the best views of the island. Cartaromana is well-known for its natural hot thermal water springs that spill out onto the shore, allowing tourists to swim in the sea even during the winter;

✓ Marina dei Maronti: Barano

At 3 km, this beach is the largest on Ischia and can be reached by taking a charming panoramic road that starts in Barano and descends towards the sea, or by foot via the picturesque port of Sant'Angelo. Another great way to reach the beach is to take a water taxi (€3 euro approx) from Sant'Angelo. The beach at Maronti is full of thermal springs, natural spas and fumaroles;

✓ Spiaggia degli Inglesi: Lovely small beach located in Ischia, suitable for enjoying a peaceful rest, far away from crowds;

✓ Cava grado: small cove located near Sant'Angelo; hydrovolcanic activity occurs in outpourings of hot water which can be used for relaxing baths. To get here, there is a steeply sloping foot-path starting at Succhivio;

✓ Bagnitiello: series of sandy beaches along the sea front road, equipped with car parks and bathing establishments;

✓ Sorgeto: Sorgeto is a shingle small bay, in Panza, lying at the foot of cliffs covered by agave plants. Here thermal waters gush from springs into the sea. On the hill behind, is an important archaeological site, known as Punta Chiarito, which was where the first Greek colonist planted vines and a hut village.; and

✓ Fumarole Beach This beach is supposed to be the island's finest. It's long, wide, clean and not too crowded; it's also of a dark colour, since it's of volcanic origin. It can be reached in 30 minutes by taking a footpath from Sant'Angelo, or in a couple of minutes by boat-taxi. There are some fumaroles here, and locals often go there and cook dinner in the sand. The beach is also a popular hangout at night.

Events

One of the many things that make Ischia such a great place to visit is the variety of events from musical events and festivals to the handicrafts markets in the historical center and sports events. In spring and summer, the various villages organize several events: many of them religious festivals, which are an important part of the island's tradition and cultural identity.

Festa della Ndrezzata April: Easter Monday The *Festa della Ndrezzata* is held in the village of Buonopane, near Barano every Easter Monday. The *Ndrezzata* is a typical island dance. It is a kind of rhythmic, violent and picturesque fight where the dancers are dressed in traditional island costumes and fight each other with wooden swords;

- ✓ International Festival of Classic Music May October Forio: The first edition of the festival International of "Classic" music: a series of concerts that were held in the churches and the basilicas of Forio;

✓ Foreign Film Festival June: A cinema festival with premieres and retrospective themes dedicated to European films, especially Italian. Ischia, for example, has used as a location of Italian films from the 1950s onwards. These include the films Vacanze a Ischia with Vittorio De Sica, the colossal Cleopatra with Richard Burton and Liz Taylor and the more recent film The Talented Mr Ripley with Matt Damon and Jude Law;

✓ Vinischia July: An event that is entirely dedicated to food and wine and Campania regional crafts. It has been organized each summer since 1999 at Torre Guevara at Ischia Ponte. Shows, concerts and dances are organized around the exhibitions and the food and wine tasting;

✓ Festa di Sant'Anna 26 July; The Festa di Sant'Anna in Ischia Porto is held each year in the borough of Ischia. On that occasion, there is a sea parade of figurative boats from the island's various boroughs and also from Procida, under the Castello Aragonese. The parade ends with a prize-giving ceremony and fireworks. The festival is watched by an enthusiastic public;

✓ Settembre sul Sagarato August and September; This is a festival held every year since 1988 in the village of Piazzale Battistessa, opposite the Church of San Pietro. The festival lasts for two weeks and is filled with painting exhibitions, parades of traditional costumes, wine tasting, fagiolate (bean stew tasting), concerts and shows; and

✓ Ischia White Night (La notte Bianca a Forio d' Ischia) 24 December; Museums, churches, shops and restaurant stay open while the Ischia Notte Bianca stages music, dance and theater events.

Island Trips by Boat

An trip around the island of Ischia by boat allows you to see the coast-line that otherwise is not visible. Boat tours leave from Forio, Ischia, Sant'Angelo, Lacco Ameno and Casamicciola. If leaving from the port of Sant'Angelo, sailing westwards you can see the *Elephants Grotto* then in front of you there is a deep inlet which is low and sandy in one part and in others high and rocky which continue until you reach Punto Chiarito, passing the beaches of Cava Ruffano, Cava Grado and the *Green Grotto*. At Punto Chiarito there is the *Bay of Sorgeto* with its *hot water and muds*.

Then the coast-line becomes very high, deeply articulated, with rockfaces, precipices, recesses and promontories of: Capo Negro, Punta Pilaro, and Chianare Spadaia with its rocks like the Boat Rock, until you reach Capo Imperatore with its *lighthouse*. At first the coast-line is high and steep, then it drops and there is the long and winding beach of Citara. Then it rises softly towards *Punta Soccorso* and Forio. Passing the coast-line is low and sandy opening onto the beach of San Francesco, which laps the offshoots of Monte Caruso. Here the coast-line is high bare rockfaced, jutting out, then curving inwards before arriving at Punta Caruso and Punta Cornacchia.

Between Punta Cornacchia and the offshoots of Monte Vico, with its point of the same name, there is the delightful *Beach of San Montano*, and Lacco Ameno. Lacco Ameno is noted for its characteristic *rock of tufo*, shaped like a mushroom. Along the coast there are the houses of Casamicciola Terme. A little farther along there is Punta Scrofa with the *English beach*, then the bay of Ischia Porto. Past Punto Molino formed from the lava flow of the Arso, there is the Pescatori beach, from here you can admire the island with its castle and the Aragonese bridge. After the bridge there is an inlet for the *Cartaromana beach*. In the middle of the sea *the rocks of Sant'Anna* emerge, and going southwards is Punta Pisciazza.

The section of the coast that concludes the southern side of the island is high, rocky and marked by the promontory jutting out of Punta Lume, Punta Parate and Punta San Pancrazio. On this side of the island there is the *Mago grotto* and other grottos. From Punta San Pancrazio the coast-line continues for a few kilometers until Capo Grosso: This stretch of coast-line is commonly known as *The Scarrupata*. After another small stretch of coast-line there is the beach of Maronti, where the small island of Sant'Angelo can be seen, which was the starting point of the round trip of the island.

Charter

If you do not mind splurging while visiting the area, you can charter a yacht from one of the local brokerages, such as Silver Star Yachting . The area is ideal for holidays afloat you can go to the nearby Naples and Capri as well as to other islands in the vicinity. There are plenty of pristine beaches, hidden coves and snorkeling spots in the area.

A Trip to Monte Epomeo

Arriving at Fontana by foot or by riding a mule you can reach the peak, which is about 800 metres above sea level. Monte Epomeo is an enormous rock of tufa, in which rooms of an ex hermit and a church which is dedicated to San Nicola (recently restored) have been carved into its sides. During the day the view is marvellous, you can see the whole island of Ischia, Capri and the bay of Naples. At night you can see the town of Forio in a candid light, like an oriental city with the stars slowly fading into the sea, and dawn slowly breaking with its famous green ray.

Buy

In every village there are streets where you can go exciting shopping for craftsman ships, agricultural local products. The Boutiques, that sell *the Famous brand* clothes, mark the shopping route:

- ✓ In Ischia you can go to Via Roma, Corso Vittoria Colonna, or to Borgo di Ischia Ponte, a very nice place full of artisans, shops, restaurants and jewelers;

- ✓ In Casamicciola, the main streets for shopping are the Seafront and the adjoining Marina Square;

✓ In Lacco Ameno the seafront (nowadays called Corso Rizzolihas) been very famous since the fifties. It starts at Piazza Santa Restituta where the locals like to gather;

✓ In Forio, thanks to the large size of the town, there are a lot of possibilities for shopping. Included here are the main streets:

✓ In Serrara Fontana, do not miss Sant'Angelo, the coastal area of the town, for shopping and social life;

✓ In Barano which is also the commercial centre, is the square that faces the wonderful beach of Maronti.

Handicrafts

Ceramics making and decorating is an ancient art. This tradition has been handed down through the centuries, developing new techniques and producing a wide variety of different objects. Ceramics include objects dedicated to two main categories: objects for domestic use, such as dishes, pots, small decorative sculptures, and objects for the building industry such as tiles for paving, roofing tiles, pipes, bath tubs and so on. Terracotta is made of common clay and contains many iron impurities. Assyrians, Babylonians and Egyptians used to dry products of this kind in the sun. If it is baked in an oven, it will become dark red, assuming the particular colour known as terra-cotta varying in intensity as in relation to its chemical composition. It is suitable to be covered by transparent glazes which seal the pot and make it bright and smooth. Usually it will then be painted and decorated in many different ways. On the Island the main example of ceramics production is represented by the old workshop Mennella in Casamicciola or Taki in Forio: the workshop as well as a large exhibition of products are accessible to visitors. All around there are small pottery workshops.

Eat

It is not possible to know if it is because of that mountain that climbs towards the sky giving the idea of an island-not-island, or because of the mixture of land and sea that Ischia has kept that primitive and wild feeling that now meets modernity . For all this reasons this island is a priceless place, especially for the taste. It is an land island. Staring from the rabbit, always cooked in terracotta baking-pan with a clove of garlic, wine, little tomatoes, lard and local spices: poor ingredients for an old and very savoury dish.

Indivisible from the Ischitanian rabbit is this very savoury main course that is served with the very simple but very rich rabbit sauce. In latest years the pit rabbit became like a totem for the island. The rabbit is bred after the old manner. It lives its natural state: wild, in woods and mountains, and grows up (as for many centuries) in pits and only feeds with wild grass.

Snails are picked along the dry walls (parracine) and in woods. They are cooked in the traditional way with wild grass, especially in the internal par of the island.

An appetizer or main course (if served with mozzarella cheese), Ischitanian Caponata directly originates from the typical *insalata cafona* (peasant salad). The peasant used to eat it for lunch, in the countryside, during the working time. Nowadays there are many recipes, the oldest one combines little tomatoes, onion, stale bread or *freselle*, salad and wild grass.

Fish in Ischia does not disappoint. There are many ways to buy it fresh, directly in fish-shops or at the *paranza*(trawler) when fishermen come back from the sea. Typical of the island are macaroni with sea food, linguine with sea-urchins and different species of local fish served in many ways: marinated, cooked in the oven, with spaghetti. The paranza fry is very famous: a lot of fried little fish of different species depending on what fishermen found. Usually they bring basses white breams, giltheads, little tuna, crayfish, calamari, squids and langoustes that enrich the menu of restaurants and agritourisms.

Some passionately fond, produce honey made from bees wax, citrus fruits or flowers. The local honey has a consistency and a taste very different from the others.

There is a town between Barano and Serrara Fontana called *buonopane* (good bread). Here they have been making bread for centuries. Cooked only in wood ovens it is kneaded with the *crisc'to* a natural yeast of acid mother paste. The bread is still kneaded by hand, and its smell in the morning is stirring. All over the island. All over the island there are ovens making bread.

The rural culture is confirmed by the cultivation of many kinds of vegetables, potatoes, eggplants, peppers, courgettes, artichokes and garden rockets.

The legume are very good: lentils, chicklings, beans (they have curious and unusual varieties called *pipers* purple red coloredand *fascists* with black nuances).

The volcanic soil favours the growth of tomatoes. They are picked up in clusters and twisted to create the typical *pendoli*kept in dry and fresh place.

Of course you'll also find all of the regional specialties (such as the origianl Mozzarella cheese) from Campania served on the island.

Drink

On the Island of Ischia, the viticulture has millenarian origins. The cultivation technique is like the Greek traditional one. In fact, it is different from that one used in the middle of Italy and in the rest of the Campania province. From the coasts to the steep mountain slopes is where the vine is cultivated on proper terraced fields. Here is a list of the most famous and diffused kinds of grapes, all cultivated in the island from about 300 years ago: White Grapes Biancolella, Forastera, and Arilla S. Lunardo; Red Grapes Guarnaccia and Pedirosso o Pere e Palummo.

✓ Limoncello After a traditional meal mainly based on fish, it is very common in the Campania region to drink limoncello, usually after coffee. Limoncello is a traditional spirit distilled from lemon rinds, typical of Naples, Caserta and Ischia. It is a natural product, usually home-made from rinds of local lemons which are characterised by their large size and thick peel. Limoncello is made by steeping lemon rids in alcohol and by adding water and sugar. It is usually served chilled as an appetizer or digestif. It is also mixed with champagne and white wine to prepare cocktails. How to make Limoncello Ingredients: 2kg of lemons, 1 l alcohol, 2 l water, 1 kg sugar. Put lemon peelings alcohol for 21 days in a dark place. Then boil sugar and water. When cooled add to lemon-alcohol, mix, filter peelings and fill into bottles..and the Limoncello is ready!

✓ Ischia Bianco Doc The soul of Ischia soul is not the sea, but farming and wine growing, once in fact an area of 3,000 hectares (now 800), was devoted to this main activity. Thanks to its commerce in wine, Casa d'Ambra was founded, with its premises at the port, making history in wine on the island and in southern Italy. DOC Ischia is among the oldest in Italy : it goes back in fact to the mid 1870s and covers the whole island. The vine heritage is quite varied and includes grapes such as Biancolella, Forastera, Grape Rilla, San Lunardo, Coglionara and Falanghina.The tendency has always been for table wines to accompany either seafood or land-produce dishes. The result is a particularly elegant wine, due mostly to the volcanic terrain and dry microclimate with good thermal conditions.

Stay safe

Ischia is generally a safe destination, even for women travelling alone. The local Police are also generally friendly to women... if not always helpful. There are four main police forces in Italy: the Carabinieri (black uniform) belong to the Ministry of Defence and perform a number of different duties; the Polizia di Stato (blue tunics and grey pants) are part of the Ministry of Interior and perform general police duties such patrolling the highways; Polizia Municipale (city police) responsible for parking tickets, directing traffic, etc; and

Guardia di Finanza (grey uniforms) do customs work, but also check vehicles to make sure owners have paid proper car taxes. If you are robbed, try to find a police station and report it. This is essential to establishing a secure travel insurance claim.

The End

)

Printed in Great Britain
by Amazon

81683434R00108